[NON] HUMAN INTELLIGENCE:

AI, Automation, and How Robots Will Make Us Better People

CESAR KELLER

ISBN: 978-1-7335016-0-6

To my wife Mariana and my children Matheus and Olivia who make me a better human everyday.

ACKNOWLEDGMENTS

I am grateful to the encouragement, support, and contributions from my community of friends and family, and the ones who helped me to write this book. First and foremost, Robert Foreman, my partner on writing this book whose talent, contributions and ideas were both priceless and enriching. Steve Barbeaux and Nitesh Agrawal, star-professionals who are leading in the future of work and paving the road for all of us. Conor Morrison for his valuable contributions and deep review of the contents.

In my professional life, few leaders had a significant impact on managing their teams with real human values and yet being great achievers – Mario Fleck, Norberto Casero, Heikki Norta, and Midori Chan are exceptional ones.

I am especially thankful to a true leader who helped to shape my character, my skills and my belief in a better workplace, ruled by competence with integrity – Otto Von Sothen who has been a 21st-century leader since the 20th.

I also want to recognize all my coworkers, managers, and team players through those years who filled my life with good experiences, all essential to shaping my understanding and vision of a better future.

Cheryl Breukelman is my leadership coach for many years, formally and informally. I will always be thankful for the support and push into this new chapter of my life. Cheryl is now my partner in our new business WORK-PLACE21 and keeps helping leaders to move into the 21st. David N. Smith for believing in the project and being always on point to make contributions.

I also want to share how proud and appreciative I am to my parents for being role models of high integrity and hardworking. Also, in balancing affection and drive to have a meaningful, fulfilling life.

Finally, I want to thank my wife, Mariana. My partner in life, who always believed in the potential of this project and pushed me to do better as a leader, professional and in the most challenging role of my life, as a father.

CONTENTS

!

INTRODUCTION

I WAS TALKING WITH A FRIEND, recently, after he returned from a long drive. He said that as he traveled down the highway, he looked up from his little car at the men and women who drove the trucks he left in his wake as he passed them by. "Soon," he said, "all those trucks will drive themselves. I wonder what will happen to the drivers. How are they going to make money? There are thousands of them. Soon, no one will need them to do that work anymore. Do you know what I mean?" I said yes. I did indeed know what he meant. "For a lot of them," he said, "it's the only work they've ever done."

I did not know quite what to say. I know what I was thinking. It was the same thing I think whenever this subject comes up.

I thought my friend might want to save some of his concern for himself, and for his own job. What he didn't realize—and what so many people like him, and me, may not understand until it's too late—is that the fate of those truckers is his fate, too. To paraphrase John Donne, he should not ask not for whom the bell tolls; it tolls for him.

It tolls for me, too, and it probably tolls for you. Because the wave of automation—which will swallow up the jobs of all the truck drivers we pass on the highway, the Uber drivers who take us from here to there when we need them to, and the laborers who work in what factories have not yet been mechanized—will not stop at eliminating those jobs.

When automation comes for them, it will come for us as well. Every job is on the chopping block, or soon will be—even the ones that seem indispensable, even the ones that pay well and promise job security. We must begin to think and act accordingly.

Plans are being laid, to replace not just the forklift operator and fulfillment center employee, but the project manager and technical writer, too. Soon, computers will do those jobs more competently than human beings do them now. They will do the same work faster, without making mistakes, and they will do it much more cheaply.

The private companies that employ so many of us will soon be able to replace us with computer programs. And they will do it. There will be no reason for them not to.

A computer program can't demand a raise, or politely request one. Companies will not have to buy health insurance for their AI systems. An algorithm does not expect matching contributions to a 401(k). There is no need to replenish the supply of coffee in the break room when the ones who work for you do not eat, drink, sleep, or have bodies.

The ground we expect to shift beneath the feet of the truck driver and taxi driver is the same ground we are standing on. The sooner we recognize that, the better we can prepare ourselves for the tectonic shifts that lie ahead of us.

INDUSTRIAL REVOLUTIONS

One way we can begin to prepare for upheavals that lie ahead is to look closely at upheavals that lie in our wake—for while all of this may seem very new, it is really nothing new.

No fewer than three industrial revolutions preceded the one that is now just beginning. Every one of those revolutions caused revolutions like the ones we are witnessing, and experiencing, in real-time.

Truck drivers and project managers will be far from the first workers, and will certainly not be the last ones, to see their professions go by the wayside. In 1910, farm workers accounted for 30 percent of the United States workforce. In 2015, they accounted for less than 1 percent.[1] Middle class and upper-middle class families tend to consider having a servant in the home unthinkable, something that would be out of their reach—and strange, to boot. This is because washing machines, electric dryers, and dishwashers, among other modern conveniences, have rendered such help unnecessary. They have freed up many hours per week that we can now spend otherwise. They have made it unnecessary to hire someone to do such work, when before it was commonplace to do so.

In so many ways, our modern lives look dramatically unlike the lives that were led a century or half-century ago. This is in large part thanks to world-changing forces like automation. And while, in the short term, grand shifts in labor and economics have meant loss and hardship for many people, every revolution like this one has, in the long term, yielded a better quality of life, with dramatic increases in leisure time, and the elimination of work that is dangerous or tedious. No longer having to wash every sock you own by hand is just one small facet of this; there are countless little tasks, at home and at the workplace, that we no longer have to perform, and which have been utterly forgotten, made invisible by automation.

We can look forward to a future in which the hardest labor is done by machines, in which computers have taken on so much of what we are currently responsible for that there is hardly any need for us to work at all.

So much factory work has already been automated. We can expect that wave to sweep away all such work in years to come. The same is true of harvest mechanization; agricultural labor is almost totally mechanized, now, and it will be fully automated soon. Drones can be programmed to spray pesticides, and monitor swaths of land that are currently overseen by human beings.

---

1 Carol Boyd Leon. "The life of American workers in 1915." Bureau of Labor Statistics. February 2016. *https://www.bls.gov/opub/mlr/2016/article/the-life-of-american-workers-in-1915.htm* (accessed December 18, 2017).

One of the final frontiers of farm automation is strawberry picking; because strawberries must be handled delicately, not just any machine can do it. A company called Octinion has developed a machine that can test whether a strawberry is ripe, and, if so, pick the fruit gently without bruising it—just like a living person would.[2]

This is an indicator of where things are going, just a small taste of what's to come. And what I have to offer is a vision of what our future might look like in years to come, when the changes we are living through have taken place and we inhabit the world that follows. I am no purveyor of doomsday scenarios, and I have little patience for visions of an economic Armageddon in which no one has a job, everyone is homeless, and our children live out their lives at plasma banks and the unemployment office.

The future we need to shape is one in which we navigate the changes that lie ahead of us carefully, cooperatively, and with a concern for social equity. Developments in technology need not outpace our moral development. We can make the right choices, individually and collectively. We can live to see a new golden age.

MOORE'S LAW AND
THE ACCELERATION OF PROGRESS

It goes without saying that things are changing, and they are changing fast. Developments in technology have all but outpaced our ability to keep up with them. Innovations seem to whip past us faster than we can turn our heads to watch them fly by, and with every grand innovation it grows harder to imagine a world without it.

It was only ten years ago that the iPhone was introduced to the world. A half-dozen iterations of the iPhone later, many of us cannot imagine life without one. Like so many people I know, I never leave the house anymore

---

2 Adele Peters. "This Strawberry-Picking Robot Gently Picks the Ripest Berries with Its Robo-Hand." *Fast Company*. September 29, 2017.
https://www.fastcompany.com/40473583/this-strawberry-picking-robot-gently-picks-the-ripest-berries-with-its-robo-hand (accessed January 5, 2018).

without using my phone's GPS. I would be all but helpless without it.

There are things we cannot navigate the world without now, but which were the stuff of science fiction two quick decades ago. Cars are learning to drive themselves. Some refrigerators on the market are described as "smart." And they are smart.

Since the advent of the iPhone, apps like Uber have altered the fabric of the world we inhabit, with taxi drivers getting edged out by Uber drivers. Uber intends, in the near future, to foist on us another dramatic change, replacing its drivers with self-driving cars. The Uber driver is a job with planned obsolescence, one that came into being specifically so that it could be swiftly automated.

I remember what it was like when online tools made it easy to make travel arrangements. It was something of a revelation. Prior to then, if I had to go somewhere for work, I would give my upcoming travel dates and destinations to my assistant, who would order plane tickets and book hotel rooms.

Suddenly, it was far easier to do that work on my own. I could go to a website, type in my destination, select a couple of dates, and that was it, more or less. There was need to bother my assistant, anymore. It took seconds, and now it's second-nature.

Speaking of assistants—this is a subject worthy of a brief tangent. When I started working, every manager had a personal assistant in the form of a living person. His job, or her job, did not pay extraordinarily well, but having an assistant made the manager more productive. The assistant served an essential role. Soon, innovations like Microsoft Word, Excel, and Adobe Acrobat made their jobs easier. Then those same tools made their jobs obsolete.

Soon enough, executives no longer needed to have assistants.

But the assistant is making a comeback. Soon, the workplace will have so outpaced our ability to keep up with it, those who remain in the white-collar workforce will be unable to do their work at all without personal assistants— but of a wholly different sort from the ones I used to have. My virtual assistant will augment my capacity to make complex decisions and solve problems, so that I can work faster and more effectively.

The personal assistant is coming back to work, and soon we will need it more than ever before. The new personal assistant will be a computer program; powered by artificial intelligence, this virtual person will amplify our cognitive capacity, and point us in better directions through power analytics. Computers will not only drive our cars, but will shape our agendas, decision-making, and moment-to-moment behaviors.

Five years ago, virtual assistants, drones, cloud-based software, and artificial intelligence were limited to labs. Hackers could not conceivably bring down a whole power grid, the way they could today. Things were different.

Every indication is that progress will only continue to accelerate, to a point where the human brain not only cannot keep up, but cannot adapt.

This is not fantasy. It is pure statistical projection. Given how quickly technological developments have accelerated in prior decades, it only stands to reason that this trend will continue. As Moore's Law tells us, computer processing speeds double every eighteen months. Computers have already come an incredible distance, in the last fifty years; machines that once occupied entire basements performed far less efficiently, and less capably, than the phones we carry in our pockets.[3]

---

3 Big Think Editors. "Big Idea: Technology Grows Exponentially." The Big Think. http://bigthink.com/think-tank/big-idea-technology-grows-exponentially (accessed January 3, 2018).

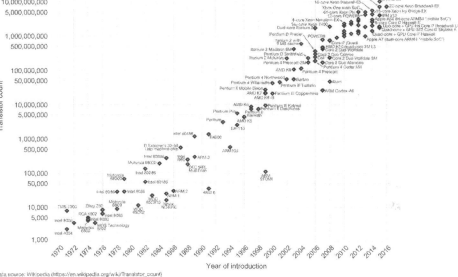

Figure 1. Moore's Law
Source: Max Roser

Such a thing could hardly have been foreseen by those who came before us, and developments will arise that we cannot yet conceive of. Things that sound outlandish to us now will be ordinary. We will take them for granted. The coming age, and its technologies, are a tidal wave that has not even begun to sweep over us. We must prepare ourselves for it.

THE URGENT NEED FOR SOCIAL EQUITY

It would be hard not to acknowledge that, so far, the revolutions as we have experienced them have not brought on increased social equity.

In recent years, the gap between the rich and the poor has grown. It's less of a gap, now, than a chasm. It is widening still, to make a canyon.

People have lost their homes. Wealth has not trickled down; it has flowed upward in a torrent.

The effects are both material and not. As we lose social equity, people lose money, and spend more of their time and energy trying to keep their heads above water. They lose the capacity to care for one another, to do the work of sustaining themselves and others. Poor people have fewer things, but the greatest loss is the loss of one another. When you spend all of your effort merely treading water, you can't help buoy up someone else.

It does not have to be like this. The changes to come need not exacerbate inequality. They can, in fact, help to end it.

While the political climate, at any given time, may seem to make this impossible, it is hard to deny what automation has done in the past. It has provided us more leisure hours, and helped make our livelihoods more sustainable. Technology, on the whole, enables us to have a better life. It brings convenience. It means there is more wealth to be distributed. When there is no need for anyone to do the sort of labor that we currently do, it means we can have more free hours to care for one another and to educate ourselves.

But every wave of technological change—every industrial revolution—has disrupted lives. It has caused pain and suffering. Ordinary people have lost jobs or businesses, and they have had to be re-equipped to keep pace with a new system, usually through higher education and specialization.

What is unique about our current sea change, the Fourth Industrial Revolution, is the time we are being given to adapt to it. With the first three industrial revolutions, people had decades to be reskilled and reeducated. They had years to relearn how to do their jobs. But with our revolution, the one we see playing out right now, we will have far less time to get up to speed with what is new. And this makes for a dire situation, since we live on the brink of the most profound social inequality of our recent history.

This is not about coal miners, embedded in a mountain range, out of sight, losing their way of life, or truck drivers having to suck it up, when their trucks drive themselves, and learn how to use Microsoft Office.

Millions of office jobs, in years to come, will be eliminated. The World Economic Forum estimates that five million office jobs are at risk of being eliminated before 2020 ends.

That is just the start. Salaried employees who go to work from nine to five, five days a week, with defined routines, will see their jobs disappear in less than a decade.

Even jobs that involve significant human interface can be outmoded by computers. The remaining jobs will require complex problem solving, critical thinking, creativity, and strategic and systemic thinking. It will only be a matter of time before they are gone, too.

Take the world of finance, in which workers must make complex decisions based on knowledge and intuition; it might be hard to imagine many jobs in a sector like that being done by computers. "Yet," write Michael Chui et al., "about 50 percent of the overall time of the workforce in finance and insurance is devoted to collecting and processing data, where the technical potential for automation is high." Half of the tasks done in the insurance and finance industries are simple, requiring no complex thought. These tasks can easily be done by artificial intelligence. And they will be.

When half of the work done in finance can be automated, it will be automated. This means the elimination of entire career paths, and it is by no means limited to finance. Insurance workers, managers, and real estate agents will see their jobs utterly transform or disappear in years to come.[4]

The middle class is in danger of disappearing, as jobs disappear, and the jobs that take their places pay less. Workers will be left out of the economy by developments in technology they can hardly be reskilled in time to master.

We must begin to think seriously about how we can best venture into the future that is shaped by the changes that are currently underway. This book is one effort to do exactly that. In the pages ahead, I will present a vision of the world that can be ours, and the good things that can come into being if

---

4 Michael Chui, James Manyika, and Mehdi Miremadi. "Where machines could replace humans—and where they can't (yet)." McKinsey & Company. *https://www.mckinsey.com/business-functions/digital-mckinsey/our-insights/where-machines-could-replace-humans-and-where-they-cant-yet* (accessed January 5, 2018).

we make the right choices today.

There is no guarantee that automation and other effects of artificial intelligence will ring in a better world, marked by social and economic equity and shared prosperity. If anything, looking at the way things are now, that future may seem comically unlikely.

But things do not have to get worse. Our failures as a society need not be permanent fixtures of the world we live in. The rise of automation doesn't have to be the death knell of the middle class. We can leverage these changes in the favor of everyone, guarantee that innovations reflect our ethics, and make decisions that promote, rather than corrode, social equity.

The world to come can be more of a paradise than a dystopia. But we need to make decisions now that will help bring it into being. In the pages ahead, I will offer a vision of the future I see and demonstrate why, despite all the bad news, we are headed for a new golden age. I will offer a vision of a future that is nearer than we may now realize, and which we have it in us to bring about.

CHAPTER ONE:

Everything Is Fluid

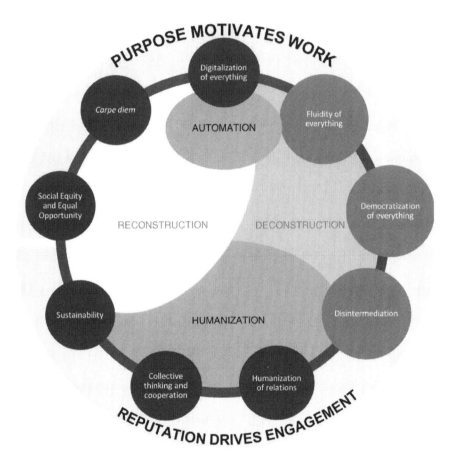

Figure 2. Trends
Source: CollectiveBrains

THE PERIOD AHEAD WILL BE ONE in which truths we have internalized and things that have long been familiar to us deconstruct and reconstruct in forms that are altogether unfamiliar. Everything that can change will change, including how we look for work and how we do our work, once automation and artificial intelligence have revolutionized the workplace.

The figure above represents graphically the complex transformation that is at hand, and serves as a kind of roadmap to this book and the thinking that underlies it.

Purpose will motivate our work. Reputation will drive our engagement. These two things will be expanded on in chapters of their own; suffice it to say, for now, that they are two of the most notable coming developments, especially in a word where commuting to work is no longer necessary, and work so frequently happens online.

That is one enormous way in which our work has largely already changed; thanks to the technologies we enjoy, we don't need to pack ourselves into little offices, or even big offices, and breathe the same air and take up each other's space as we get things done. As many benefits as there are to doing that, most people would prefer to manage their own space, to work from home or, anyway, not have to travel to someone else's office for so many hours of every week. And so, thankfully, that is what many people are doing.

At the center of the wheel, we have the forces that are driving these changes: Deconstruction and Reconstruction, which are bound together; and Humanization and Automation, which are two sides of the same major trend. As we will see in Chapter Three, as automation takes effect, we will be put back in touch with what makes us human, with what makes for a good, fulfilling life of meaningful work and contact with others.

And at every point in that broad circle, we see the principles that hold all of this together. The work of the future will be sustainable. As information and resources grow more accessible, democratization takes effect. All of these principles will be addressed at length in the pages ahead.

At the heart of this book, though, is the realization that we need to come to terms with what the future will bring. Automation will mean that work that takes up so many hours of labor today will be done by computers, freeing us up to work with and for one another.

In the economy to come, purpose motivates work. Reputation drives engagement. These principles are the guardrails of the future of work.

When people no longer work simply because they have to—when we do it with something in mind apart from, or in addition to, sheer sustenance—the nature of work will change. Our ultimate goals will supersede the immediate ones. We will never lose sight of what we are working toward, the future we build together and the community we partake in.

When so much work is done collaboratively and remotely, working online and engaging with one another from a distance, reputation will become supremely important. The establishment and maintenance of a good reputation will keep us in the workforce, and ensure our high performance. We will know our reputations. They will be quantified for us. We will work hard and work well in order to keep our reputations clean, and we'll do it for the sake of maintaining our places in a grand community of workers, which will ensure that the community functions well.

We will all work well with others. We will have to. Our standing in the working world will depend on it, even more than it does now.

COOPERATION, EDUCATION, AND EQUITY

This book is concerned with the changes we face and the speed with which they are changing. It is also about the constants we would do well to recognize, as we witness and survive those changes.

There are truths we should be made aware of again, values that we can and should embrace in the years to come.

One of these is the need for cooperation. In the modern workplace, by and large, competition is the great motivator. We do, of course, work together; we function as members of teams, and work toward a common goal. At the end of the day, though, we are far more interested in our individual well-being than we are in working with others. We compete for promotions. We work to sustain ourselves, and work with others in the name of serving ourselves as individuals.

That approach to work will be one of the casualties of the Fourth Industrial Revolution. When the work we do now is no longer done by human beings, people will be called to engage in different sorts of work altogether. We will collaborate. We will cooperate. We will put our heads together, and the new technologies will help us do it.

Education, too, will help us accomplish our goals. The need for us to be educated is a constant. It is how we ensure that we make good decisions— politically, nutritionally, environmentally, and otherwise—and it is necessary for us to foster a sustainable world, in the face of climate crisis and overpopulation.

It will be necessary for us to be educated in an ongoing, continuous manner. With the imminent wave of automation, we will have more time to engage in this necessary, sustaining work.

Education is one powerful means for achieving greater social equity, which should be our greatest concern as we face the changes ahead. We will see greater social equity in the years to come. Despite the losses people have suffered and are bound to suffer, the result, in the end, will be greater equality among us and more fulfilling lives for us to lead.

Again, it can be a little hard to believe in this, sometimes, given the growth in wealth inequality and wage stagnation. But a look at the past tells us a great deal about the future. In the early twentieth century, only about 18 percent of the American populace had finished high school. Most jobs did not require any education whatsoever.

While the world we live in today is far from perfect, most people in the United States do attend and finish high school. Continuing one's education into college has become commonplace. These are promising developments, indicators that the lives we lead are better than the lives our great-grandparents led. And one of the reasons for this change having taken place is that—thanks, in part, to automation and the economic shifts that accompanied it—young people are not being pulled out of school so they can do high-risk work as farmhands or factory workers.

If we extrapolate this trend into the present moment, it only stands to reason that the hours we see liberated in years ahead will mean more time for us to continue educating ourselves, bettering ourselves, and keeping ourselves relevant to an ever-changing economy. It means that while it may be disorienting to see the world we live and work in slip away, it might be for the best that our world is changing the way it is.

The turbulence we pass through ahead will be worth it. On the other side of it lies a better life for us all.

It is all too easy to be discouraged by developments in the immediate present. News arrives with frequency that offers quite a lot of discouragement, whether it tells us of a wildfire or a spike in unemployment, a natural disaster or one made by human hands. But we cannot lose sight of the direction we continue sailing in, despite the choppy seas that buffet our ship.

We can turn the new industrial revolution to the advantage of the many, not the few. We need not leave anyone behind. If we venture into our shared future in a responsible, morally sensible fashion, we can make the developments ahead work for everyone.

THE TELEPHONE AND THE TELEGRAM

Like everyone else, I watched, in recent years, as telephones virtually disappeared in favor of cellular phones. Cellular phones were replaced, in short order, by smartphones, which changed the very nature of a phone and what we expect one to do; we rely on our phones, now, to do many times the work they once did.

It can be discomfiting, to say the least, to watch things change, as technologies we take for granted deconstruct and reconstruct anew. I rarely even speak into my phone anymore. It speaks to me, and I speak to it. It gives me directions when I drive, and soon I will not even need it for that, for I will not need to drive. My car will take me where I need to go, with minimal input from me.

Just as we have watched telephones as we once knew them go the way of the telegram, and just as getting lost while driving is becoming a thing of the past, entire professions have diminished in importance, if they have not gone by the wayside altogether.

Whereas it was once a thriving profession, one that many people could not live without, people now forego, for the most part, booking flights and hotels through travel agents. Why not, instead, simply go to one of many websites that do the same work instantly, and at a fraction of the cost? It's hard not to feel bad, when you think of it, for the young travel agents who must have been entering the profession in, say, 1995. But now that we have Orbitz and Travelocity, Kayak and Priceline, the near-elimination of travel agencies seems all but inevitable.

The same thinking that takes nearly every one of us, in the modern era, to an online flight-and-hotel-booking service, rather than across town, to the office of a travel agent, is the same thinking that will only continue to eliminate jobs that have been traditionally held by workers in the middle class. It is not in our interest to pay extra money and take more time to reach the same result we could achieve by paying less and spending almost no time whatsoever. Nor would it make sense for a profit-seeking company to pay a human being to do the same job a machine can do better and at minimal cost.

Everything is fluid—meaning, all rigid structures that are still standing will soon be blasted by the digital revolution. We are, as a society, in the process of eliminating data asymmetry and creating transparency. Governments, corporations, educational institutions, and more, will be transformed, and we will all feel the effects of this process.

A report emerged from the executive branch of the US government, in 2016, stating that a job paying less than twenty dollars per hour had an 83 percent chance of being automated in the near future.[5] Jobs that pay more than that will be automated, too, like the jobs of tax preparers, insurance underwriters, data entry clerks, and telemarketers.[6] It would be hard to compile a comprehensive list of jobs that will be automated, as so many of them are slated to disappear in this way. Reports on the coming wave of automation proliferate; a quick Google search will turn up dozens of them, and the only things they seem to disagree on are the precise numbers— exactly how many millions of jobs will be eliminated or changed irreversibly in the near future.

The theoretical physicist Stephen Hawking wrote in *The Guardian*, in late 2016,

> The automation of factories has already decimated jobs in traditional manufacturing, and the rise of artificial intelligence is likely to extend this job destruction deep into the middle classes, with only the most caring, creative or supervisory roles remaining.

> This in turn will accelerate the already widening economic inequality around the world. The internet and the platforms that it makes possible allow very small groups of individuals to make enormous profits while employing very few people. This is inevitable, it is progress, but it is also socially destructive.[7]

---

5 Ryan Vlastelica. "Automation could impact 375 million jobs by 2030, new study suggests." *Marketwatch*. December 4, 2017. *https://www.marketwatch.com/story/automation-could-impact-375-million-jobs-by-2030-new-study-suggests-2017-11-29* (accessed January 1, 2017).

6 Patrick Scott. "These are the jobs most at risk of automation according to Oxford University: Is yours one of them?" *The Telegraph*. September 27, 2017. *http://www.telegraph.co.uk/news/2017/09/27/jobs-risk-automation-according-oxford-university-one/* (accessed January 12, 2017).

7 Stephen Hawking. "This is the most dangerous time for our planet." *The Guardian*. December 1, 2016. *https://www.theguardian.com/commentisfree/2016/dec/01/stephen-hawking-dangerous-time-planet-inequality* (accessed January 12, 2018).

In the age in which we find ourselves, nothing can be taken for granted. Everything is in flux. Our jobs are in peril—but so is everything else. It is not only the modern American workplace that stands to be shaken like an Etch A Sketch and redrawn. Institutions that seem or seemed unshakeable have been or will be shaken, too. Established power structures are subject to tremendous change.

This is due, in large part, to the availability of information, the revolution in dissemination of knowledge that the Internet has brought us, which rivals the invention of the printing press in its implications.

Rigid power structures are held in place by the asymmetry of information. Other people claim ascendancy because they know more than we do—because they have access to knowledge that we do not have. Once information becomes more available, more accessible, that asymmetry is threatened.

Availability of information is what the Internet, and the countless innovations it made possible, have brought us. The invention of the Internet may not have meant an instantaneous smashing of current social orders the world over. But thanks to the new digital age is has rung in, the ice has begun to crack.

There is no more dramatic instance of this I can cite than the Arab Spring—the popular uprisings that swept the nations of the Arab world and unseated regimes that had stood for decades.

Years after the protests and ousters have taken place, enough time has ensued that we can see the aftermath, which is uninspiring at best, and horrifying at worst. It is hard to celebrate the Arab Spring with untroubled enthusiasm, or to hail the accomplishments of that moment, without lamenting the violence that followed in countries like Egypt and Libya.

But events that seemed unthinkable, for years—the deposing of dictators, and the dramatic overturning of the status quo—were facilitated by social media. They were made possible by the use of Twitter among protesters. They helped make possible the disruption of power and end of oppression.

With the introduction of technology that gave people access to Twitter and other means of communication, dissenting voices could reverberate as never before, shaking to the foundations structures of power that had seemed indomitable. A whole global region was thrown into disarray, thanks, in no small part, to the sudden wide availability of information that digital technology made possible.

With its inherent fluidity, social media—which changes constantly, based on who is using it, and on what new content is introduced to it—overwhelmed concrete and seemingly unshakeable totalitarian rule.

This is the way of things, now; we should look on the Arab Spring not in isolation but as part of a much broader trend. Everything is changing in the direction of being less rigid. We can see this trend in enormous uprisings like the Arab Spring. We can see it on a smaller scale, too, in the effects of the employment website Glassdoor.

GLASSDOOR AND THE RISE OF TRANSPARENCY

Glassdoor is, in so many ways, like any employment website. It is where, if you are looking to hire someone, you can post an ad. If you are looking for a job, you can go there to find ads for job vacancies. In these ways, it is what we have come to expect from sites like it, over the years—except that Glassdoor has an additional and potentially revolutionary feature. It invites current and former employees at a company to review that company; to give it a star rating and provide feedback; to write a review of a workplace as if it were a restaurant.

It may seem, on its surface, like a small thing. It is no small thing!

Its implications are vast. It completely changes the dynamics of a job interview, by giving knowledge of a workplace to anyone who wants it, particularly those who are considering joining that workplace. If a company's values do not accord with those of a potential employee, or if it seems, on the whole, like an unpleasant place to work, then the prospective employee will know to keep away. It gives a job seeker knowledge that, before a site like Glassdoor, they would not know until it was too late.

Glassdoor is a means for putting toxic workplaces on notice—to make companies that depend on hiring competent personnel take seriously the question of whether their workplace culture is hospitable or not. If a tech company is run by negligent managers, then that is bound to come out in the reviews of those who have moved on to greener pastures. If a consulting firm takes the idiosyncratic measure of requiring its employees to clean the restrooms they share on a weekly basis, to cut cleaning costs, then that will be the first thing anyone reads about when they look up the company on Glassdoor. It will have an effect.

The effect will not, of course, be that no one will work for the offending company. There is too much demand for jobs for that to be the case. But it will mean that that company cannot hire the best people, or the people it wants— and that can have dramatic, long-term effects on a company's prosperity.

Glassdoor is a mechanism for sharing information among those who need it and have trouble getting it—those who are seeking to secure an income for themselves, or to find a better job in a workplace they consider more suitable or hospitable. It allows those who stand outside a company to see it through the eyes of those who are or have been on the inside. It makes it possible for someone being interviewed for a job to interview the interviewer—to arrive at an interview with more than self-knowledge and an eagerness to take on new challenges in a new setting. Through the sheer availability of information—and the willingness for regular people to share information amongst themselves—a playing field we must all perform on gets a little closer to being level.

In the example of Glassdoor, we see digital technology promoting the kind of cooperation that we need to engage in more and more, as we see existing power structures crack and even begin to crumble. Glassdoor itself does not provide us with information about a company, beyond what that company provides in its advertisement for a job vacancy. What it provides, most crucially, is a forum for us to provide information to one another. It invites us to collaborate on piecing an accurate portrait of a company. We offer our impression of a workplace, and as others offer their insights as well we give a prospective employee an accurate sense of what it would be like to spend their working days in that setting. We are not paid to do this; we do it because we recognize it as a worthwhile thing to do.

We recognize, too, on some level, that we stand to benefit from this kind of cooperation. We know that as employees—as subordinates to the employers—we are not in power. We are shut out of the rooms where big decisions are made that affect our lives. As often as we are encouraged to compete with one another, for jobs and promotions, cooperation comes far more naturally to us. A site like Glassdoor serves to remind us of this.

It reminds me of something else, too; in fact, watching the advent of Glassdoor has felt a little bit like déjà vu.

Early in my working life, I was employed by a company called Accenture, at an office in Brazil. I was one of many young, educated people who were employed by the company. All of us were smart and motivated. We had bright futures ahead of us.

The workplace was like many others, with power in the hands of partners and managers, and employees like myself who were left mostly in the dark. A rigid structure was in place, to dictate who would advance in the company, when, and how far. Annual promotions and salary increases were based on performance, and information on how well or poorly we performed was in the hands of management.

The environment at Accenture was fiercely competitive, when I began working there, the way workplaces so often are. The phrase we used to describe the culture was "up or out." You moved up, or you were out.

It was simple. It was cold.

All of us did our best, and collaborated when we needed to. But we guarded our accomplishments carefully, and, at the end of the day, made sure to take credit for as much as possible, in the name of beating one another to the next raise and/or promotion.

Then a fairly groundbreaking thing took place. Those of us who worked for the company began sharing amongst ourselves the feedback we had been given by management—our performance reviews, and the promotions and raises we had been given.

We gave one another the opportunity to compare how we had been treated by management. With more information in front of us than we had ever had before, we could determine for ourselves what seemed fair and what seemed right.

We conferred with one another. We brought our findings to our managers, and made it clear to them that we recognized the unfairness of the situation at hand.

The result was not a total undoing of the workplace power structure. The managers were still the managers. We still worked for them. We knew where we stood; we knew the score, and a revolution was not what we were after. What we wanted—and what we achieved—was for the managers to have to take into account, when they made decisions, our increased awareness of the total situation. They had to be more mindful of us at every step. If they made a decision that was patently unfair, giving promotions where they were undeserved, or not recognizing someone's achievements, they knew we would know it. The dynamics of power were not overturned completely, but the asymmetry of information was corrected slightly, just enough to make a palpable difference to those of us who were subject to it.

When Glassdoor came into being, I recognized exactly what the website was doing. I knew what its effects would be. The same changes that took place in my workplace in the 1990s could happen on a much larger scale, with input coming in from a vast array of people.

A tool like Glassdoor has the potential to fundamentally alter the way hiring is done. It puts a company's reputation in the hands of employees and former employees. It gives power to those employees. We have only begun to see the effects of such a tool.

THE #METOO MOVEMENT

As I write this, the #metoo movement has been at work for some months and shows no sign of slowing down. And I cannot help but wonder, what better, more potent example could there be, of the sharing of information pulverizing established structures of power and domination?

Rumors had swirled for years about rampant sexual harassment and assault in Hollywood, business, journalism, the tech industry—virtually everywhere—until women began speaking out about harassment and sexual assault on social media outlets like Twitter, which provided the forum for women to share their stories readily and fuse them together with the hashtag they used in common. Many people had known all along that sexual assault and harassment were pervasive, and that they inflected the lives of women in profoundly negative ways. The proliferation of stories on Twitter made this undeniable to those who might otherwise deny it, and provided a necessary education to those who were surprised by the revelations.

Much attention has been drawn, too, to the online spreadsheet that was contributed to by various women who had suffered abuses at the hands of powerful men. It was offered up as a space in which women could report what they had endured, and at whose hands, as a means to warn women who were on their way into a given industry of the perils that lay ahead of them. Once the spreadsheet was made available, according to its creator, contributions to it poured in, in the name of cooperating on behalf of those who needed information in order to survive in their chosen fields.

Its initial purpose was to share information among those who needed it, to warn women of the hazards that lay ahead of them as they made their way into their careers. From these developments have come investigations, resignations, and public reappraisals of some of the worst offenders.

The movement began with the sharing of information. The results have included the breaking down of longstanding power structures. In the words of the spreadsheet's creator, Moira Donegan, "I had imagined a document that would assemble the collective, unspoken knowledge of sexual misconduct that was shared by the women in my circles: What I got instead was a much broader reckoning with abuses of power that spanned an industry."[8]

This is all to say that the developments we see play out and will see play out are not altogether negative. It can seem utterly terrifying, on its surface, that artificial intelligence is getting so sophisticated that many of the jobs we have will disappear before new ones are created at scale. It should mitigate our fear, to see new technologies bring on changes that are undeniably positive.

Things have always been in flux. People have always taken things to be solid and immutable that are anything but, and it has always been the case that things we take for granted are subject to change.

Think of how the railroad utterly transformed transportation, and made a trip across the United States a matter of weeks and not months. Think of how the automobile brought on a dramatic change in the transportation infrastructure of countries worldwide.

What digital technology has done is accelerate the rate of change. It has put new demands on us, in that we have less time to adapt to the unfamiliar. In the words of Heraclitus, "Change is the only constant in life." And it is not enough to say that we should embrace it. We *must* embrace it.

There is not one universal truth that cannot be revised or rewritten. That has always been true. What is altogether new is how plain and undeniable this has become, how we are made to look that reality in the face.

THE NEED FOR ONGOING EDUCATION

We must take seriously our need to be educated on an ongoing basis—to make education something we pursue and engage in at every step of our progress through our careers. At a time when we can expect to have the rug pulled out from under us, again and again, it is essential for us to know where we can safely plant our feet.

---

8 Moira Donegan. "I Started the Media Men List." *The Cut.*
https://www.thecut.com/2018/01/moira-donegan-i-started-the-media-men-list.html
(accessed January 10, 2018).

Based on the what we can observe from the last time technology revolutionized our economy, three types of skills will be in high demand in the next couple of decades: professional skills, transferable skills, and affective skills.

We can expect, in the coming years, for professions to merge. We will watch as they consolidate, two or more entire fields becoming one, across the professional landscape. This change will require us to be proficient in not just one area of expertise but two or more.

Take, for example, the legal profession. Before long, there will be no need for paralegals and junior counselors; digital tools have made their jobs easier, and will soon make them unnecessary.

Veteran lawyers will not be any more secure in their positions than their colleagues were. Lawyers will need to have computer science skills, so that they can create new algorithms that will help them put their knowledge and skills to work. It will not be enough to be a good, well-trained lawyer who is consistently in practice. It will be necessary for a lawyer to know how to make that expertise translate to the fully digitized and mostly automated modern workplace.

When robots are able to master small surgeries and replicate them at scale, research doctors will need mechatronic skills to develop and test new procedures. It may sound like science fiction, but robots are already being enlisted in performing minimally invasive surgeries, and their further involvement is around the corner[9].

College students should be aware of this dramatic shift in the workplaces they hope to enter. It is not enough to declare a major or field of study; the workplace of the near future calls for a combination of fields of study, an overlapping expertise in several areas.

Indeed, the changes that lie ahead of us demand that we rethink education—that we emphasize creativity and interpersonal skills, rather than

9 Mayo Clinic Staff. "Robotic Surgery: Definition." *Mayo Clinic.* https://www.mayoclinic.org/tests-procedures/robotic-surgery/basics/definition/ prc-20013988 (accessed January 23, 2018).

relying on the acquisition of knowledge or practical skills[10]. Workers in the near and distant future will need to have skills that carry over from one field to another.

This is in part because most of the intellectual work in the future will be developed collectively. Collaboration, communication skills, and teamwork will be critical to every job, no matter what area it is in. Those skills will be essential for us to perform in new environments, most of them virtual, and get things done alongside others. We will explain, later, the need for more collaboration, and skills that will facilitate it.

Most middle-class jobs—in management and supervision, and countless miscellaneous office jobs that defy categorization—will soon disappear. We will look back on the last few decades and wonder how anyone did it, laboring in a cubicle, alone with a computer, with someone checking in on her once or twice a week. It will appear to us to be a physically safer but no less soul-killing version of sending children to spend their short lives to work in factories.

The jobs we leave behind, at those isolated desks that no one in his or her right mind will miss, will be replaced by jobs in which we spend our time in the presence of others, physically or virtually. We will work together as a rule. Collaborating well with our peers will no longer be something that helps us secure a good job; it will be the most fundamental skill or ability necessary to secure any job. Having compassion and empathy will be prerequisites as important for being hired as having the right skills.

Even the most competent medical doctor must have a good bedside manner; so it will be for all the rest of us, who will need to know how to couple our skills with the ability to work with others.

---

10 Harry A Patrinos. "The implications of automation for education." *The World Bank.* *http://blogs.worldbank.org/education/implications-automation-education* (accessed January 23, 2018).

ZILLOW, REDFIN, AND
THE CHANGING FACE OF REAL ESTATE

If I wanted to buy a house tomorrow, my first move would not be to contact a real estate agent, as it would have been ten years ago, or more recently than that. I would not need to rely on a real estate agent to know what houses were for sale in the neighborhood I wanted to move to, or what they were being sold for; to know when it was last sold, and for what; to know what school district a house was in, and what sort of taxes I would have to pay if I lived there.

There was a time when this information wasn't readily available, when you had to be in a certain line of work in order to know it. If you wanted to find these things out on your own, it would take time. It would cost money.

Now, all of this information, and images of houses to boot, are readily available on apps like Zillow and Redfin, which compile real estate information that, in the past, it would have taken significant effort to find. There were gatekeepers in the way of this information. Now they are gone.

The new technologies have made looking for a house into a new kind of pastime, something to be done on your phone or tablet while you wait for your name to be called at the doctor's office. Now that looking for a house need not take up the time of a realtor, and can be done in private, without commitment, it can be fun, or at least diverting.

The name for what has been happening to real estate is disintermediation. There is less and less need for intermediaries, which means it is less necessary all the time to pay fees to the ones who once held the keys we needed to access the market. When we don't have to pay those fees, the market can grow. We save time and money.

Apps like Zillow and Redfin are only the beginning. A startup in North Carolina called First is the next stage in the transformation of real estate. Their algorithm analyzes hundreds of data points that are relevant to a given homeowner—such as a change in income, the loss of a job, a recent divorce filing, or the birth of a child—to determine whether someone is likely to want to sell a home. When a new baby comes, a couple might want to sell their two-bedroom house. If a married couple divorce, they might want to buy apartments. First compiles and processes this information in order to help realtors predict our behavior. They give realtors a kind of sixth sense for when a homeowner wants to put her house on the market. Realtors can stop distributing magnets and junk mail, in the hope that we will see their magnets and junk mail at the right time. Instead they can show up right when we want them to be there, as if they had been summoned.[11]

It can be a little unsettling, to consider the implications of this technology. It can seem like something out of Philip K. Dick—like the short story "Minority Report" (and film of the same name), about a police force that attempts to stop murders before they happen, except with real estate sales.

It isn't an outlandish concern. That this technology is being put to use means that someone out there who is looking to make a buck has a computer that consolidates scattered information about you, making complex analyses and predicting your behavior, whether you like it or not. The information they use is publicly available, but their use of it is nosy at least, and not necessarily in your best interest.

On the other hand, this is not dramatically different from what I experienced when I bought my first house: one by one, financial advisors dropped by to leave me their cards and let me know they were at my service if I needed them. I had just bought a house, and so they knew I must be doing well enough to have finances to advise, even if I had no interest in what they offered.

Technology like First's works in reverse—it is predictive, and not reactive—but its effects are only as harmful as having strange guys in ties appear at my front door, wanting to manage my finances. If a dramatic event takes place in my life, one that would lead me to want to sell my house, First could not force me to sell my house; they would only make it easier for someone to find me,

---

11 Matt Hunckler. "This Real Estate Startup Uses Data Science to Predict Home Listings Before They Happen." *Forbes.* December 20, 2017. *https://www.forbes.com/sites/ matthunckler/2017/12/20/this-real-estate-startup-uses-data-science-to-predict- home-listings-before-they-happen/* (accessed January 24, 2018).

if her job is to help me do that. And the company's technology has a rather democratizing effect on the real estate market, making it possible for smaller realtors to compete with larger companies that have traditionally had access to more information and better resources.

Whatever your opinion on their technology in particular, a company like First gives rise to certain worthwhile ethical questions, the likes of which we should consider, discuss, and thoughtfully answer before the new technologies are fully integrated into our lives. If we wait long enough, it will be far harder to consider those questions, let alone do anything to really address them.

SOCIAL MEDIA AND THE NEW GOLDEN AGE

This book as a whole considers what is perhaps the largest ethical question we face in the current era: whether we should—and whether we have it in us—to bring on a new golden age, given the advances in technology that are at hand.

It is incumbent upon us to put our new technologies to use in ways that benefit as many people as possible, that do not exploit us or our fellow citizens, and that make our lives better, rather than worse.

This may come across as intuitive—as a statement so obvious it hardly warrants articulation. But ensuring that we promote equity, fairness, and safety as we bring new technologies into our lives is exactly what we have not done for at least the last ten to twenty years.

Like so many other people, I watched in the last decade as social media went from essentially not existing to being a central part of our everyday lives, seizing an ever-greater share of our mental and social energies. It began as a curiosity; I remember logging on to Facebook and being, in a word, amused. It was fun, for a little while, and before I knew it, it was a website I went to several times a day. It became some people's preferred means of reaching out to me; soon I had to go there, if I wanted to be in contact with certain friends I had in distant places. It never was my preferred source of news; for that, I go to online newspapers. But I would be lying if I said that I never read an article that was linked through Facebook. I would be lying if I said I didn't probably read one every day that was linked through Facebook, starting I don't know when.

All of this took ten years or so. Social media was a pool a great many of us eased our way into, in this way, and it wasn't until we were fully submerged that we found the water was not as safe as we thought it might be. It wasn't until social media was integrated into our lives that most of us learned that it had been the site of propaganda, that it was a means for other people to steer our thinking in one way or another. It wasn't until Facebook and Twitter were integral parts of our lives that we watched congressional hearings in which our legislators tried to come to grips with the extent of the influence of these inventions on our thinking and our politics.

By that point, social media had become something we could hardly pry ourselves away from. Even now that former executives have said publicly that looking at Facebook isn't good for us, and it has been investigated as a possible means for thought control by foreign agents, it is hard to imagine everyone leaving it behind.

Imagine how differently this could have gone if everyone had known what social media was capable of in, say, 2007, when Facebook and Twitter were still fairly new. Regulations could have been put in place; users might have known not to let their children spend too much time on them. They could at least have understood what they were getting themselves into—what the side effects might be, of handing over so much contact with other people to private companies.

Those people are not exactly living in a dystopia shaped by social media companies; it isn't like that. But they do know—many do, at least—that Facebook and Twitter are in their heads, in ways they did not expect when they first signed up for them.

Artificial intelligence will be in our heads, and will influence our lives, in ways that are far more extensive than that. It is imperative that we reckon with it now, before it has taken over our human resources departments—

to take one example—and decides whether we should keep our jobs or lose them. Data is being put to use in novel ways, in order to make businesses more productive, efficient, and profitable than ever. As Chelsea Allison wrote recently, for *Legion*, we will see labor management decisions being made based on far more precise metrics than ever, such as

> the item-level sales, the foot traffic, and even real-time external drivers like local events and weather. After all, these factors are what's really driving sales, so they should also be what really drives a proper labor forecast. For example, sporting events can drive alcohol sales for a restaurant, so it would be great to be able to identify this precise demand and staff bartenders accordingly when an event's happening (as opposed to, for example, hostesses and servers). Or, because foot traffic forecasted at an hourly level is a better insight into labor than sales, retailers can use that info to maximize conversion opportunities and ensure that there are enough people at the front of the house.[12]

All of the decisions that might be made based on this information involve reducing the need for labor and letting go of employees. If we multiply the effects of these relatively small-scale changes by the number of businesses in the United States alone, many of which employ thousands of people, it is not hard to imagine how the more extensive use of data could revolutionize our economy.

Technologies in development now promise to have sweeping effects on how we live and work. There are hard questions we should ask before we feel those effects in full.

Everything is fluid, and all things are in flux—but that doesn't mean we cannot impose some order on the chaos, and work to ensure that when the dust settles we are better off than we were before the upheaval began.

---

12 Chelsea Allison. "Why you're probably doing labor forecasting wrong." *Legion*. March 28, 2018. *https://legion.co/why-youre-doing-labor-forecasting-wrong/* (accessed July 9, 2018).

THE ETHICS OF NEW TECHNOLOGIES

Let us return to First, the company that processes a vast number of data points and uses them in order to learn whether or when you will want to sell your house, for the benefit of real estate agents who stand to profit from your intention to put your home on the market.

One of the life events that First considers, when attempting to determine whose house is or is not slated for sale, is death. Of course it is. When people die, their houses are often sold off by their survivors. If, when I die, a computer program tells a realtor that she may want to get in touch with my children, to help them deal with the house I have left behind, I have no problem with that, honestly. If anything, it may make the process a little simpler for them.

Consider, though, that in the near future we are likely to have wearable computers monitoring our vital signs at all times, and communicating with concerned entities and institutions about how we're doing. If I have one on, and I have a heart attack, it can alert the nearest self-driving ambulance, and deliver a living or robotic paramedic. My life can be saved. The wearable computer could even communicate with the office of my primary care doctor, alerting them to less dramatic maladies, like a steady increase in blood pressure. The office's AI can prescribe me blood pressure medication, when I reach a certain dangerously consistent level, or at least tell me I ought to go and see the doctor in person. It could schedule me an appointment.

Given this, the wearable computer could see a heart attack coming months in advance. It could know, because of my blood pressure, my diet, and my refusal to exercise, or even take a brisk walk now and then (in this future, I have become dangerously sedentary), that I am doomed. A stroke, or something, is imminent.

Who will it tell, the device that I carry on my wrist? It may tell my doctor, who may implore me to come in for a checkup. It may tell my grocery store, which will send alerts detailing the healthy food I can go and buy there, or have delivered via drone.

Will it, though, tell my insurance company? And would the insurer, knowing that I was given warnings about my health, withhold benefits from me, on the grounds that I was given warnings about my behavior, which I ignored? Could an insurer get away with reneging on a life insurance policy, knowing that I knew that death was a likely outcome of consuming only steaks, milkshakes, and Oreo cookies?

When my wearable computer sends the alert to my doctor and insurance company, it might also send a message to First, to alert them to the strong possibility that the house I live in will soon go up for sale. The device could tell the human resources department, at the company I work for, that they may want to prepare to post an advertisement for my imminently vacant position. It could direct Facebook to begin advertising to my friends companies that prepare flower arrangements, as they'll likely want to send them to my family soon. My friends will not know why they're seeing these ads, but when I die they will know just what to do.

These scenarios are distasteful at best, outright exploitative at worst. They are ways to derive maximum profit from death. A technology that has clear and admirable virtues turns sour when it signals to the vultures that they should begin circling over our heads. These are hypothetical scenarios, but they are likely to be absorbed into the daily reality we take for granted.

And it could be that there is nothing wrong with these possible outcomes. It could be that, once we have had informed debates about these things in a public forum, we decide that we want coffin manufacturers to know how many of us are not taking care of ourselves, so they will know what sort of sales they can expect in the next year.

I want, though, for us to have this debate, to have these conversations amongst ourselves, so that we can begin to articulate the limits of how far we are willing to go with these technologies, what degree of invasion into our lives we want from them. Because if we do not have those conversations, they will be had all the same—but we will be left out of them. We will leave it to profit-driven companies to decide how to use the technologies they invent. And while they may be well-intentioned, on the whole, and led by conscientious people who are sensitive to invasions of privacy and exploitation, they will be locked in fierce competition with other companies, and will have to sacrifice such concerns for the sake of their survival.

This is not inevitable, but it is the sort of thing we have seen take place with other technologies. And the stakes, this time around, are far higher, given that artificial intelligence promises to inflect virtually every dimension of our lives.

We have to talk about these things—with one another, with our representatives in government. There are hard conversations we must have, before it is so late that it is nearly impossible to regulate the new technologies.

It is our habit, as a society, to let a new technology establish a beachhead in our lives and remain there, growing in its influence until it affects as much as it is capable of, and then finally get around to questioning it when it has already begun to cause serious problems. Falsified journalism is easily passed off as legitimate; rideshare platforms hire drivers without vetting them, inviting abuse of a system that asks passengers to trust the people who ferry them about; search engines collect data on the people who use them, and sell that data to advertisers, who use the information to try to extract as much money from users as they can. By the time something like this has taken place, it is hard to seriously question the role the technology plays in our lives, what share in our daily experience it should have. It is already there, and it is very hard to remove or minimize it.

It is deeply ironic to me that as a country we are made to wrestle constantly with questions concerning immigration. Often, we hear politicians and public figures ask what will become of us if we let more immigrants cross our borders. If we allow a certain number of refugees from Syria, Iraq, or Honduras into the United States, how will it affect those of us who already live here? What will be the effect on our taxes, our jobs, our culture, and our children? And yet when a new technology comes into being, we embrace it with our arms wide open, asking none of the same questions, which are far more relevant when it comes to something like artificial intelligence, which stands to upend our economy in ways no living newcomers to this country, no matter their numbers, possibly could.

It reminds me, too, of what it was like when cellular phones made their first appearances in our lives. For the most part, people seem to understand that when they go into a movie theater, they need to silence their phones. Before every movie, a message appears on the screen to remind us all to do it. But it took years for those messages to finally appear. It took years for everyone to get into the habit of setting their phones to silent when they went to movie theaters.

Again and again, we have let digital technology outpace our need to control it, or our ability to establish social mores to help us govern their use. We introduce powerful new things without determining in advance whether we should try to contain them, without establishing rules for them. We cannot afford to have the same approach to the innovations to come. They are far too potent for that.

And if it seems as if I am being hyperbolic, if it is hard to imagine a new technology exceeding our widely held expectations for it, then that, too, is consistent with what we have experienced in the past. As a rule, technology defies our expectations for it. New developments arrive without us seeing them coming. No one knew, in the late nineties, what a profound role the Internet would play in our lives in years to follow.

When I worked at Nokia, around 2002, the company had the greatest share of the worldwide mobile phone market. Everyone used phones to make phone calls, and so the effort was always to make phones smaller, and easier to carry around. There were those who said that the trend would reverse—that phones would start getting bigger. We would not use our ears when operating them, but our eyes; it was how people articulated, at the time, the dramatic shift we now know as the development of smartphones. Most people didn't take this seriously, and before too long Nokia would lose its place at the forefront of development in this area.

WHERE WE SHOP AND
HOW WE ARE WATCHED THERE

At the time of writing, Amazon Go has just opened its first supermarket, in Seattle. It has been in the news, and now everyone knows that to shop there you need not bring a wallet or go to a checkout. You grab what you want and go. Amazon will charge you automatically.

Meanwhile, an array of sensors and cameras monitor you, to see how you interact with Amazon's products—to see if you walk toward a product, if you pick it up and inspect its nutrition information and put it down, or if you breeze past it without giving it a first or second glance.

When I worked at Frito-Lay, we did this sort of thing with human observers, watching people as they ventured into supermarkets to try to determine how they went about deciding whether to buy something, and what to buy. But there is no need to use people for this anymore; Amazon's cameras pick up everything, and their computers process all of the information you give them—via facial expression and body language—automatically.

Using this information, Amazon—and any company that does something like this—can market to you more aggressively something you seemed to consider buying but didn't. They can charge you more for something you did not hesitate to buy, on the grounds that you probably need it or want it enough to be willing to pay a higher price. And they can more efficiently make something you might like to have into something you think you need. If you seem to consider buying a more upscale and expensive form of granola than you're used to buying, they can tell you in a promotional message that it's available at a lower price, which they have tailored to you. Then, when you have bought it a few times, the price might abruptly go up again, because at this point you have come to expect to eat that granola every morning.

Any place we go to shop is a place where we are being manipulated, somehow. Window displays are old-fashioned ways to make us want things we don't need, to entice us into purchasing things we would not otherwise think to spend money on. Amazon Go takes that to the next level. It doesn't use a window display; it makes the shopper into the thing that is observed. It uses digital technology to probe us, to better learn our preferences and desires, so that Amazon can more efficiently separate us from our money.

And it is important to have big data in mind whenever we consider these things. Whatever Amazon learns about us through our body language at the Amazon walk-in store is, potentially, added to the already substantial mass of information that has been collected via search engines, social media, online shopping carts, Apple Pay, and on and on.

When we consider the implications of the technologies of the present and of the future, we must have in mind this swirling mass of information that rotates over our heads at all times, which of course, in fact, is stored in a data farm somewhere. The scale of what is known about us compounds any ethical dilemma we will need to consider.

AI AND FACT-CHECKING

Artificial intelligence has much to offer us. Some of the innovations it is likely to yield are undeniably good in a way that is fairly plain. It promises to change the way we work, the way we're trained for jobs and are hired for them. It is also likely to bring us a new way to fact-check in real-time.

Whatever an individual's political persuasion, he or she is likely to agree that little to no good can come of people being led to believe things that are not true. It is wrong for politicians, in debates and public appearances, to lie to us. Some of us know when a politician is lying, but much of the time, while we may hear what a public figure says with a skeptical ear, we do not always know an untruth when we hear one.

Imagine a televised debate in which a bar appears on the screen that turns green when a candidate is telling the truth or stating an opinion, but glows red when that same person says something that is found to be untrue—or a ticker that treads across the bottom of your TV screen, citing statistics and data that help to indicate whether what someone has just said has any objective truth in it.

At the moment, fact-checking is a laborious process that can only really be done after the fact; by the time a lie can be proven false in a heated debate, several more lies are likely to have been spoken, or the attention of the debaters and their spectators has turned elsewhere. By thinking and working faster than those who seek to deceive us, AI can help us to protect ourselves from untruths and preserve us from demagoguery.

This is just one of the innovations that AI will bring into our world that can have overwhelmingly positive effects on the lives we lead. It should indicate just how beneficial AI can be when it is used to our collective advantage, and how imperative it is that we ensure it is used properly.

POSTCAPITALISM

Everything is fluid, down to the very fundamentals of our economic system as we know them. Artificial intelligence promises an upending of the way we work and live so dramatic that many modern thinkers are convinced that the way we do business—or business itself—is due to be rewritten.

Among them is Paul Mason, whose book *Postcapitalism* presages a time, in our near future, when capitalism simply cannot sustain itself. Mason takes a close look, throughout his book, at postindustrial towns that were ravaged as industries departed, taking the jobs they provided with them. He concludes that things cannot continue as they have been.

Even more important than these plain realities is the technology that is on its way. "But the technologies we've created," he writes,

> are not compatible with capitalism—not in its present form and maybe not in any form. Once capitalism can no longer adapt to technological change, postcapitalism becomes necessary. When behaviours and organizations adapted to exploiting technological change appear spontaneously, postcapitalism becomes possible.

Mason argues that although capitalism is by its nature an adaptable system, there are certain technological realities it simply cannot adapt to. Capitalism is predicated on restriction of information, on knowledge being unavailable to some and closely guarded by others. That is simply not a reality that will last long into this century.

Mason calls for some rather dramatic changes in the face of what he sees as the inevitable end to capitalism: socialization of the financial system, something like a universal basic income, and public ownership of healthcare, housing, energy, and telecommunications.

I do not follow every aspect of Mason's argument through to the end; I do not see an end to capitalism in the near future, but a certain transformation of it. But he is certainly right to see on the horizon some dramatic changes that are to come, specifically in that power structures cannot sustain themselves as they always have in the face of freely flowing information.

And while I may disagree with some of the particulars, an argument like Mason's seems to me to be just right in its spirit. We have entered an era in which we must question the future of everything, even those things we have always safely taken for granted, like the most fundamental principles of our economics. We have to be willing to picture a near future in which so many things are deconstructed and reconstructed and made nearly unrecognizable. It is essential that we picture this new world, if we are to have any hope of knowing how to live in it.

Those who have done some of this work include Steve Denning, who, writing in *Forbes*, posits that we are living on the cusp of a new phase of capitalism, what he calls the Creative Economy, which is characterized by a newfound propensity for sharing information, but which is still driven by free-market capitalism and retains many of our current economy's extant features. Responding directly to Paul Mason's declaration that capitalism is waning, Denning asserts that it is here to stay, only in a new form.[13]

In *The Washington Post*, law professor Feng Xiang has written that AI could be a dangerous tool in the hands of oligarchs, a mechanism for exacerbating

---

13 Steve Denning. "Is Capitalism Ending?" *Forbes*. July 20, 2015. *https://www.forbes.com/sites/stevedenning/2015/07/20/is-capitalism-ending/* (accessed July 9, 2018).

wealth inequality. But it could also be used to essentially perfect socialism: it can "supplant the imperfections of "the invisible hand" while fairly sharing the vast wealth it creates," meaning that "a planned economy that actually works could at last be achievable."[14]

Everything is changing. Everything is fluid. It is up to us to adapt to those changes.

As we have said, change is nothing new. But artificial intelligence is altogether new, and we have seen nothing quite like it before. It is uncertain, at this point, exactly what direction AI will point us as we hurtle forward into our collective destiny. There is no doubt, however, that in the very near future AI will be the force that steers us.

We have to understand the current state of things, and know that the way things are is temporary. If we are to ensure that we achieve greater social equity, and make the world fit our sense of ethics, we have to see opportunity in the shifting landscape, and try to turn the tide of our fluid world in our favor.

---

14 Feng Xiang. "AI will spell the end of capitalism." *The Washington Post.* May 3, 2018. *https://www.washingtonpost.com/news/theworldpost/wp/2018/05/03/ end-of-capitalism/* (accessed July 9, 2018).

CHAPTER TWO:

Purpose Will Motivate Our Work

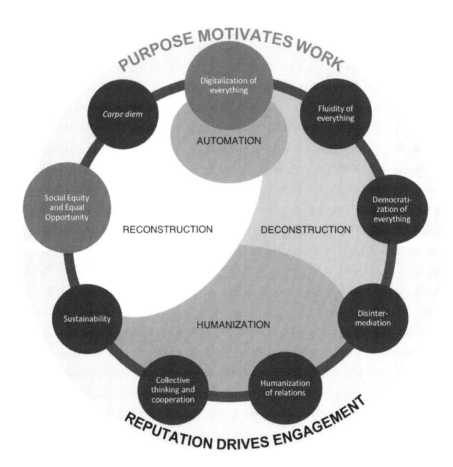

Figure 3. Trends
Source: CollectiveBrains

THIS BRINGS US TO ONE of the developments to expect from the Fourth Industrial Revolution, one of the great benefits of seeing our work utterly change in its nature. As Figure 3, the roadmap to this book, indicates, one of the underlying principles to the trends we can expect is that our reasons for working will change. The things that get us out of bed in the morning will be different things. More than material gain, more than basic sustenance, a sense of purpose will motivate us to work.

The Second Machine Age, a book by Andrew McAfee and Erik Brynjolfsson, makes the case that we are living on the cusp of a social transformation on the order of the Industrial Revolution of the early nineteenth century, when modern life as we know it began to come into being. After centuries of gradual, steady growth, the human population exploded, because suddenly the human race no longer had to rely on the mere muscle power of people and livestock in order to grow food, travel, or build things. With the perfection of the steam engine, and technologies to follow, the path of the human race was irreversibly redirected.

And now, argue McAfee and Brynjolfsson,

Computers and other digital advances are doing for mental power—the ability to use our brains to understand and shape our environments— what the steam engine and its descendants did for muscle power. They're allowing us to blow past previous limitations and taking us into new territory.

As their book attests, the things that lie ahead of us cannot be predicted with 100 percent accuracy. The kinds of changes that are taking place differ from what we saw 200 years ago, in that it is the work of the mind and the body, and not the body alone, that is being automated. But they make a convincing case that in the twenty-first century we will see our lives transformed in ways that are as sweeping and revolutionary as what took place in the nineteenth century.

It would have been impossible for people born in, say, 1820, to predict what sort of changes they would see in their lifetimes. The railroad would alter the landscape and completely change the way people traveled from place to place. Factories, driven by new engines, would draw massive numbers of people from rural settings to cities. In those factories and elsewhere, so much human labor was replaced with the work of machines.

And so, it is safe to say, the wave of automation our digital age will bring—to jobs like truck driving, office management, and so many more professions—will not be the first such wave.

McAfee and Brynjolfsson spend a great deal of their book on the workers whose jobs stand to be automated in our transition to the next machine age—the drivers, the project managers, and the forklift operators—and they offer this sobering vision without even taking into full account artificial intelligence, and what it promises to bring into being. Even as recently as 2014, when their book was first published, the technology had not advanced far enough to offer a clear view of what was to come, of how AI promises to revolutionize our work and how we do it.

As I have mentioned, it will not only be the data entry clerk at a large insurance company, whose job consists of many repetitive tasks performed competently and consistently, who will see their job done by a computer in the near future. Soon after that person goes, the claims adjustor will follow, as will the manager of the office where both of them work, and as will the person who oversees all of them.

It may be the case that these higher-paying jobs with greater responsibilities demand complex decision-making, interaction with others, and the processing of many forms of data. For that reason, they may seem automation-proof. But what they do is exactly what AI will do so well—far better than humans currently do it, and for far less money. With the introduction of AI, computers become thinking machines that can do the same work as human beings. They do it as efficiently and competently as they currently do simple math problems for us, when it's time to do our taxes—which is to say that they do it far faster and more reliably than we can.

The scale of automation of the Fourth Industrial Revolution seems vast enough without taking AI into consideration; only when we do take it into consideration can we begin to contemplate its reach. It will shake things up, certainly, but it will do more than that. It will change the nature of work. It will make us rethink not just *how* we work, but *why* we work.

A NEW SENSE OF PURPOSE

In the age to come, we will work, but our reason for working will be different. Whereas we currently work because we have to—because in the United States, at least, there is little to no social safety net or alternative to working at least forty hours per week—we are likely to see a future in which work is something we do because we believe in what we are working for. We will get to decide not just where we work—something many people currently have little say in—but *why* we work. We will decide what we are working toward, and there will be no mistaking the importance of that labor, beyond the immediate need to keep ourselves housed and fed.

This is a grand shift that will characterize our future, and which will be a feature of the age to come, but we can already see the stirrings of it in the younger generations, a remarkable change in the ways in which people see the work they do, or the work they look forward to doing as they begin their careers. A survey of recent college graduates from 2015 found that 60 percent of them said they would prefer to work for a company with a "positive social atmosphere," and that they would be willing to be paid less than they would otherwise in order to meet that preference. Only 15 percent of those responding said they would prefer to work for a large corporation.[15] This is

15 Jeanne Sahadi. "Where do Millennials want to work? Not at corporations." *CNN Money.* May 12, 2015. *http://money.cnn.com/2015/05/12/pf/millennials-work/index.html* (accessed February 8, 2018).

remarkably different from the attitudes of older generations, and it indicates how things are in the midst of changing.

In this way, millennials are ahead of the curve. For so many reasons, it is right that they should not want to work for large corporations—one of those reasons being that the corporate jobs will be automated out of existence sooner than many others. It would be hard to understand the shift in attitudes from the older generations to the millennials without taking into account automation, and the revolution it promises.

The millennials can see that revolution coming. A recent survey by Udemy found that among millennials and Generation Xers, stress in the workplace had gone up 44 percent and 33 percent, respectively. The number one cause of that stress, among respondents, was the (well-founded) fear that they will lose their jobs to automation.[16]

The second reason respondents cited for increased stress was "bad managers"—which, of course, can mean anything, from unethical behavior on the part of those managers, like wage theft, to bullying, to negligence. Anyone who has worked in an office knows the harm a bad manager can do, and has an idea of how many bad managers are out there.

The good news is that the number one thing that stresses out younger workers will help solve the problem of the second most stressful thing in their working lives. Thanks to the automation that keeps them from falling asleep at night, their horrible bosses will lose their jobs soon, too, making way for altogether new kind of workplace that is coming into being. It will be far less susceptible to the folly of poor management, and generate far less stress for those who are in it, who will be unified by a sense of shared goals, and not divided by a sense of competition.

---

16 "Workplace Confidential: The Real Story Behind Stress, Skills, and Success in America." *Udemy for Business.* https://business.udemy.com/blog/workplace-stress-study-infographic/ (accessed February 8, 2018).

MILLENNIALS AND PURPOSE

Recent studies of the inclinations of the millennial generation have observed that they want to be engaged in purpose-driven work. As we've established, they tend to prioritize it far more than their parents did, and consider it more important even than material gain.

And so, if millennials appear to some to be uninterested in hard work, or to have a work ethic that does not conform with their parents', it is wrong to conclude that something has gone awry, that they have the wrong values. It can be easy to judge a whole generation by the wrong metrics.

"They want to feel like they are making a difference," writes Ahmad Raza. "Yes, they love money, but millennials need to know they're making an impact, even if it is a small one."[17]

Karl Moore, at *Forbes*, backs this up. Millennials, he explains, "are constantly seeking purpose in what they do for a living and at the same time want to know how their job is helping them get to the top." They are not attracted to a career solely because of how well it pays. They want to work for a company that knows where it is going, and they want to know for certain what its role is in generating a better future. "Organizations," Moore writes, "who wish to prosper will focus more time on meaning at work, have an organizational purpose and contribution which gives people a sense of satisfaction and a genuine feeling that they are making the world a better place."[18]

There is a great deal of truth in all of this. Millennials do have a different attitude toward work than their parents do. They are motivated to work by the need and desire for money, but they take the cause they work for into account as they choose what to do and where to devote their many hours of labor.

---

17 Ahmad Raza. "Why a Purpose-Driven Mission Is Key to Motivating Millennials." *Entrepeneur.* December 12, 2016. *https://www.entrepreneur.com/article/284857* (accessed February 8, 2018).

18 Karl Moore. "Millennials Work For Purpose, Not Paycheck." *Forbes.* October 2, 2014. https://www.forbes.com/sites/karlmoore/2014/10/02/millennials-work-for-purpose-not-paycheck/ (accessed February 8, 2018).

But analyses of the younger generation's work preferences tend to treat this new development as something that millennials turned to on a whim, as if a whole generation of people simply decided they would be unlike their parents—an enormous mass of people suddenly, collectively preferring to pursue sustainable careers.

Those analyses tend to leave out the conditions that have helped bring on this prevailing mentality. Because as often as it is disregarded in such conversations, surely it is not incidental to millennials' turn toward meaningful employment that they have spent their lives watching climate change alter the face of the planet. They have had to take seriously, all their lives, an immanent existential threat to life as we know it, and it will be up to them to learn to survive in a world with cataclysmic weather, overheated oceans, and bleeding ecosystems.

They enter their working lives already saddled with enormous amounts of debt, from the student loans they had to take out in order to secure educations that were, by comparison, handed to their parents. They have automation in mind, too. They know far better than their parents do how fast the world is changing, and they know it will be up to them to adapt to it. Surely the change in priorities between the prior generation and theirs has something to do with this.

Rather than wonder at the difference in priorities between millennial workers and their parents, it seems more astute to give millennials credit for understanding that their working lives are set to be substantially unlike those their parents knew.

It is not so much that millennials' preferences have changed as it is that they have been paying attention. They know they will live to see work that diverges far from what their parents did. They are simply preparing themselves for it.

And while they are still, by and large, rather young, the people of Generation Z—who have arrived on the heels of the millennials—are distinct in their own ways. Even more than millennials, Generation Zers are native to digital technology; in large part because of their early exposure to it, they have a far more natural proficiency with technology in the workplace than prior generations have had. Surveys find that they are more likely to become entrepreneurs than members of prior generations.[19] Their experience of life is bound to be fundamentally different from that of, say, a baby boomer, from the way they communicate with one another to the way they look for jobs. Digital technology, and the changes that follow from it, have changed many things, and will change many more things. We can expect to see this next generation respond to those changes in their very constitution, in their identity as a generation.

There are so many questions millennials and Generation Z will have to answer, which their parents would not have dreamed of having to address, including the question of what they will do with their time once so much of the work that once had to be done by people is done by machines.

What will make them want to work? What work will they do? In a world where law firms can count on AI to scan thousands of documents in an instant to help lawyers prepare for a trial, what will become of those who would have grown up to be paralegals?[20]

How, indeed, will people pay their bills? Where will they get money to buy food?

In order to answer questions like these, it may be necessary to venture into territory that would have been anathema to American public discourse in, say, the 1950s, or even the decades that followed. Indeed, even today, when proposing options that have even a faint whiff of socialism, one must look over one's shoulder to ensure that the specter of a redbaiting member of Congress isn't prepared to swoop down and question the participants' patriotism.

---

19 Matt Kleinschmit. "Generation Z characteristics: 5 infographics on the Gen Z lifestyle." *https://www.visioncritical.com/generation-z-infographics/* (accessed February 12, 2018).

20 Carl Benedikt Frey and Michael A. Osborne. "The Future of Employment: How Susceptible Are Jobs to Computerisation?" *Oxford Martin School.* September 17, 2013. *https://www.oxfordmartin.ox.ac.uk/downloads/academic/ The_Future_of_Employment.pdf* (accessed February 8, 2018)

I am committed to capitalism. I own businesses. I am in the midst of starting a new company. I am, undeniably, a capitalist. But I hope that by this point in our history, we in this country have moved far enough past the Red Scare that we can learn the lessons that socialism has to teach us—that we can emulate, in our own way, those countries like Norway, Finland, and Sweden, where capitalistic enterprises thrive at the same time that socialistic measures are taken to ensure that no one is left out of prosperity.

We must understand, as the wheel of the Fourth Industrial Revolution turns, that socialism is not our enemy. Inequality is our enemy, and while I would not accept a dramatic turn toward socialism, a total communist revolution, I do hope that we can recognize the usefulness of adopting policies that grow out of socialism, which we can implement to our benefit.

THE PROMISE OF A UNIVERSAL BASIC INCOME

In the workplace of the future, purpose will be the basis on which we decide what we do, and how we do it. We will choose our careers because of the ultimate goals we have in mind, like dealing with the effects of climate change, or helping to reduce poverty. Solutions to grand problems, rather than hope for grand paychecks, will get us out of bed in the morning.

There are so many things people are willing to deal with simply because they have no choice in the matter—from insufficient pay to overlong hours, to unfeeling, even sadistic supervisors, to the sinking suspicion that the work they do not only doesn't benefit the community they live in, but actively corrodes it.

As it is now, if you lost your job, you would probably have to scramble to find another one as soon as you can. As much as you might want to work for a company that operates sustainably, ensures the well-being of its employees in a couple of important ways, and doesn't seem like it might work you to death, you would hardly be in a position to hold out for a job like that.

You could do such a thing, and have much less to worry about, if we had a universal basic income, if everyone, regardless of who they were, were doled out an established sum of money to help make ends meet. Relying on a UBI, you wouldn't make as much as money you're used to, but there is a chance you could wait things out and look for just the right opportunity, rather than having to settle for the first opportunity you find.

This is not something that would only benefit those who lose their jobs and must scramble to find work. It would have a ripple effect throughout our labor market; it would force employers to provide better incentives for people to come to work.

Think of the workplaces in Silicon Valley, where employees are invited to take breaks and play table tennis, and even take naps in specially made cots under their desks. These are small things, but they indicate the mentality of employers who know they must make their workplaces appealing beyond being willing to hire and pay someone.

We should expect the work we do to change as the conditions under which we do that work change. And everything is changing, now, from the climate to the labor market. We can count on things that seem impossible now to, quite soon, be real.

We must be willing to think big! Because it goes without saying that people with a great deal more resources than we do are thinking big, and they do not necessarily have our ethics or sustainability in mind, like the executives at fossil fuel companies who spent the twentieth century ensuring that our electrical and transportation infrastructure was built so as to consume their products.

At this point in time, the concept of a universal basic income (UBI) may appear to be altogether fantastical. We live in a country in which very few things are given out freely to anyone, by anyone, even if it is in everyone's best interests, and sometimes when it is necessary for the sake of the recipient's survival.

Given that, the notion of a UBI seems outlandish. It would mean giving every citizen in the United States an established sum of money so that he or she can buy food, pay the rent or mortgage, and keep their children alive, if they have them. It would mean ensuring that everyone whose job has been made obsolete by automation is provided for, when their livelihoods disappear thanks to forces that are far beyond their control.

It sounds like an unlikely scenario, this being implemented. But everything is subject to change, and many things that seem immutable will turn out to be otherwise, the further we get into the Fourth Industrial Revolution.

Besides, it would be hard not to note the growing enthusiasm for something along the lines of a UBI, and the implementation of similar programs as experiments, or trial runs.

In January 2017, Finland began distributing monthly payments of around $700 to 2,000 of its unemployed citizens, chosen at random. There were no stipulations attached to this, no conditions they had to meet in order to qualify for payment. It is too early to determine what the outcomes of this will be; interviews with recipients of this money have reported only that they are less anxious about money, and that they are better able to meet their most basic needs.[21]

The city of Stockton, California has done something similar. At the start of 2018, the city government gave several hundred of its poorest residents $500 per month, to help them make ends meet, and see what came of this support.[22] Would it reduce the recipients' motivation to work, as so many skeptics have claimed? Or would it simply improve the mental well-being of those who benefited from it?

The list of countries that have taken some form of action in the way of implementing a UBI—either contemplating it, or putting it into effect—is long. But perhaps the most familiar example of something very similar to a UBI, which has been in effect for some time, is the state of Alaska's Permanent Fund. Since 1982, the Fund has doled out a sum of money to every

---

21 John Henley. "Money for nothing: is Finland's universal basic income trial too good to be true?" *The Guardian.* January 12, 2018. *https://www.theguardian.com/ inequality/2018/jan/12/money-for-nothing-is-finlands-universal-basic-income-trial-too-good-to-be-true* (accessed February 2, 2018).

22 Alix Langone. "This U.S. City Will Give Its Poorest People $500 a Month— No Strings Attached." *Time.* January 24, 2018. *http://time.com/money/5114349/ universal-basic-income-stockton/* (accessed February 7, 2018).

established resident of Alaska. It began as a means for sharing the wealth that was generated by the oil industry, starting in the 1970s. Through it, the Alaskan government has distributed as much as $2,000 to each of the state's residents. It is hardly enough to constitute an income; it would be hard to live on $2,000 per year. But it provides a remarkable example of what is essentially a UBI, one that has been in effect in the United States for several decades.[23]

Similarly, in North Carolina, the Eastern Band of Cherokee Indians pays dividends to its members from the profits of the casino the tribe operates. They have been doing this long enough to find that the dividend payments had the effect of reducing crime and substance abuse, among other problems.[24]

With private funding, a group called Y Combinator is piloting a program in which it gives money to a hundred families in Oakland, California, with no strings attached, for five years. Writing for the group's blog, Y Combinator president Sam Altman explains, "50 years from now, I think it will seem ridiculous that we used fear of not being able to eat as a way to motivate people."[25]

Universal Basic Income is a concept that has been touted in recent years by Silicon Valley titans like Elon Musk and Mark Zuckerberg. But there is hardly anything new about it. It has been traced to Thomas More, Thomas Paine, and Milton Friedman, the economist who advised Ronald Reagan and has inspired several generations of fiscal conservatives. Martin Luther King, Jr. called for something along the lines of a universal basic income, and Richard Nixon's administration experimented with UBI in several states, finding that it did not hinder any recipient's work ethic, contrary to what so many of its critics want to warn us of.[26]

---

23 "History of Basic Income." Basic Income Earth Network.
   http://basicincome.org/basic-income/history/ (accessed February 12, 2018).

24 "Basic income around the world." Wikipedia. *https://en.wikipedia.org/wiki/Basic_income_around_the_world* (accessed February 12, 2018).

25 Sam Altman. "Basic Income." *Y Combinator.*
   https://blog.ycombinator.com/basic-income/ (accessed February 7, 2018).

26 Matthew Heimer. "A Brief History of Free Money." *Fortune.* June 29, 2017.
   http://fortune.com/2017/06/29/universal-basic-income-history/
   (accessed February 7, 2018).

If it seems strange that conservatives like Friedman and Nixon would have supported something that seems so unsuited to their overall ideologies, part of its appeal to some is that it could offer a viable replacement for government programs they look on unfavorably, like social security, or Medicare. If the government simply handed people money, rather than orchestrating relatively complicated social programs, it would mean reducing the bureaucracy—and, to entertain a more cynical thought, it would make it far easier to eliminate social programs altogether. Social security has been around for many decades, now, and people rely on it; it would not be an easy thing to end. If it were replaced with regular disbursements of cash, to everyone, then those disbursements could simply be reduced, again and again, until they were nothing. Or the allotments could not be increased to keep pace with inflation, until they become essentially worthless. In this way, in the wrong hands, something like a UBI could be a dangerous weapon.

UBI is a strange case, in that it appeals to people from varied political positions for altogether different reasons. The Movement for Black Lives endorsed it as a means for paying reparations to African-Americans. The most recent Socialist party presidential nominee in France included a basic income in his platform.

As Alyssa Battistoni has argued, in *Dissent*, "The problem with basic income is that it tends to be read as an idea without an ideology." As a concept, it appeals to very different people, for very different reasons, and because it has not been fleshed out in much detail by any one political faction or party, its hypothetical particulars are entirely malleable. One proponent might see in it a means for freeing the unemployed former truck driver, whose job has been automated, from want. Another observer might see in it a means for ending unemployment benefits and food stamp programs. On a skeptical note, Battistoni claims that

> these disagreements get to the heart of the matter. The debate about
> basic income is about the obligations we have to one another, the ori-
> gins of property, the ends of human life, the shape of our society. And
> when these broader visions are translated into policy, they don't simply

suggest a shared plan to give people money—they offer drastically different accounts of how much money people should get, where it should come from, and who should get it.[27]

This is not, however, a reason to dismiss the idea altogether. It can be encouraging, rather than dispiriting, to see the appeal that the UBI has across the political spectrum; if people from different parts of that spectrum disagree over its implementation, then resolving those disagreements is exactly what politics are for, imperfect though the political process may be.

The very fact of a UBI being taken seriously by influential people, with trials being run and interest growing, is a welcome development. When it has been tried out, it has proven to be successful; its negative effects are negligible. UBI would provide us with the means to seize that moment in which automation frees up so many work hours and ensure that some good comes of it. It would mean improving social equity right when it becomes possible to do so. It also means that we are beginning to take seriously the realities that lie ahead of us, such as the evaporation of work as we know it.

That development will require sweeping solutions to enormous problems. Robots and AI will take jobs away from living, breathing people, and they will have to have a way to keep themselves living and breathing. UBI is one possible means for pulling them back from the brink. It is one way to make our world more sustainable—which is the sort of thing we absolutely need to do, if we're to be a part of the future.

PURPOSE-DRIVEN COLLABORATION

When they are pulled back from the brink, through the implementation of a UBI or another means, and we find we are not living in a dystopia in which no one works or eats because robots stole all of the jobs, the nature of work will have changed. The workplace of the near future will be all but

---

27 Alyssa Battistoni. "The False Promise of Universal Basic Income." *Dissent*. Spring 2017. *https://www.dissentmagazine.org/article/false-promise-universal-basic-income-andy-stern-ruger-bregman* (accessed February 7, 2018).

unrecognizable to those of us who are accustomed to things as they are.

The future of work is already coming into being. Digital disruption is the norm, and new talents are busy acting, as entrepreneurs or collaborators, to bring about new ways of collaborating and creating value. New ways of engaging with work digitally are proliferating.

New networks, platforms, and job opportunities are generated by the minute. The future of work will not arrive all at once; in many ways, it is already here, even if not all of us have felt its impact.

We can catch glimpses of what the future will look like by looking at those companies that have been founded recently, and have done it with an eye to not only surviving into the future, but helping to shape the future of work.

I grew acquainted, recently, with Nitesh, a young engineer who founded indiez.io, a community of independent designers, developers, and product managers who have come together with a shared purpose. The ways in which they work together are remarkably new and totally effective.

After spending some time with traditional big tech companies and start-ups, Nitesh broke from that beaten path in favor of creating a better environment for software talent. In the name of doing that, he has formed a collaborative network that leverages talent twenty-four hours a day across multiple countries. They work fast and affordably. Their model gives their talent a greater share of the revenue their work generates. Their company works, and they get results.

Indiez can, among other things, help a large enterprise launch a product in a matter of months. A flagship case is Tikkle (Tikkle.io), a smartphone app that facilitates collaborative work among employers and employees regardless of their geography. In Nitesh's own words,

> It was one of our complex assignments. We collaborated with the Tikkle's team remotely to get to a right feature set. From a concept in their board member's heads to a real product feature set. We have brainstormed online and remotely. After, we engaged a team of fifteen members from four different time zones collaborating to build Tikkle. We

managed the project through processes like daily check-ins, weekly reviews, regular demos and closed feedback loops. We developed mobile apps, web apps, backend and admin panels. The product was very elaborated as we were building impressive designed features with high performance on low-end smartphones, integrating the best-fit third-party solutions for a chat and live streaming, and serving enterprise customers with 100,000+ users all at the same time.

Indiez uses new technologies to stimulate collaboration, nurture collective thinking and to guarantee high-quality deliverables. Using tools like Dropbox, Trello, and Drive, the people at Indiez collaborate remotely with maximum efficiency.

At a company like this, the risks of harboring divisive office politics or a toxic workplace culture are minimal. Everyone who works at Indiez works with the team toward a common goal. And it is collaboration such as this that makes way for new forms of work altogether, for work that unites us behind a common purpose that transcends material gain.

SOLVING NEW PROBLEMS IN NEW WAYS

This same way of operating—among people who are far apart geographically, but who converge virtually on a given problem with their own cultivated skill sets, and with a common purpose—has been used to address some of the biggest problems we face today. These include climate change, perhaps the greatest challenge that our species has ever faced. It is such an enormous, sweeping problem that it requires us to rethink the very ways in which we solve problems.

That, anyway, was the thinking behind the inception of the Urban Climate Change Research Network (UCCRN). Established in 2007, it originally consisted of 100 researchers operating out of sixty cities, who pooled their resources to study the growing problem of climate change, specifically as it relates to the impact on the world's urban zones. The group conducts studies and publishes work on what city leaders and urban planners can do to prepare for the climate change-related problems they will no doubt face in the near future.[28]

Researchers who work with the UCCRN include professors and researchers from universities and think tanks. They are social scientists, urban designers, and air quality experts. There are now more than 800 of them, and although they are geographically disparate, they work in concert to conduct research and develop proposals.

These people are doing much the same work they would normally be doing under any circumstances; social scientists are applying social science to understanding climate change. But rather than doing their work in isolation, and bringing it to the attention of fellow experts in their fields once the work is ready for it, they work collaboratively from the start. By working together, they can properly address a vast and complex problem, one that changes all the time. About 110 authors, from more than fifty countries, recently co-wrote the organization's ARC3 report.[29] They coordinated many hours of labor, performed by a wide array of people, in order to do this.

The way in which the UCCRN operates is how we can all expect to do our work, soon enough. Collaboration will not be something we strive for, or say we value without necessarily doing it, as is so often the case in today's workplaces. We and our colleagues will be united in what we do by a shared sense of purpose, and we will work together, despite the physical distance between us, in real-time. The technology for accomplishing this is not just around the corner, it is already here, and some are already taking advantage of it.

It is no accident that so many participants in the UCCRN are from academic backgrounds. To find a model for how purpose can be a great motivator for our work, we need look no further than the academic world.

28 "About Us." *Urban Climate Change Research Network.* *http://uccrn.org/who-we-are/overview/* (accessed March 1, 2018).

29 "Climate Change and Cities: First Assessment Report of the Urban Climate Change Research Network." UCCRN. *http://uccrn.org/resources/publications/arc3/* (accessed March 1, 2018).

Academics are perhaps the best examples we have of people who choose their work more for how important they take it to be than for how well it will pay them, or how upwardly mobile they will be in their fields, or how generally excellent their lifestyle will be. Perhaps the oldest purpose-driven workplace is the university. No one is there because it is the best-paying gig available to them. They work longer hours than many others do.

It is understood that a professor who takes a job at a research university will do several different kinds of work in the course of their duties. They will teach classes; they will mentor students outside the classroom; they will sit on committees, in their department and college, to ensure that the institution functions as it should; they will do research in their chosen field; they will peer-review the research of others, to ensure that it meets certain standards. Much of this work is not compensated, apart from their baseline salary. The most they have to gain from their work outside the classroom—which is the labor they are paid for—is a reputation at their institution and in their field. The work of peer-reviewing colleagues' work, for example, often means many additional hours of labor, without additional pay, and often without even being recognized in any substantive fashion.

So often, academics are painted as lazy or derelict people who cannot function in other sectors of society—when in fact they are among the hardest-working people around. They had to fight tooth and nail to secure the jobs they have, and they have to meet steeply competitive standards in order to keep them. They are not paid especially well; you would be hard-pressed to find, say, a science professor who could not have made far more money, and perhaps even have had an easier life, by entering the private sector.

They have chosen to walk a hard road, because they believe in the work that it requires of them. They put in long hours, and devote many years to their labor, because it means engagement in a kind of work the meaning and significance of which is self-evident to them. An art history professor, whose work is so easily dismissed in our society, does their work because they believe in its importance.

The university as we know it may change dramatically in years to come. With so much work being done online, and so much educational resources moving there as well, it may seem less and less wise to devote as much money as we do to maintaining physical campuses and dwelling in classrooms.

But we will likely see the nature of work becoming altogether more like the nature of work done by academics. We are likely to do the work we do first because we know it is worth doing, with everything else being secondary. When the terms by which we engage with the labor market have changed, so will our reasons for engaging with it in the first place.

THE RISKS OF A UBI

The Fourth Industrial Revolution will create wealth the likes of which we have not seen before. We must ensure that it is distributed equably. One way to do that would be to implement a UBI—but we must also ensure that people do not become wholly dependent on the money coming in through such a program.

In Brazil, in the 1990s, we had as president Fernando Henrique Cardoso, who used a concept like a UBI to promote social equity. He created the Bolsa-Escola, a program that gave each family a substantial sum of money for every student they kept in school—not enough to make work unnecessary, but enough to truly incentivize keeping a child in school.

The effect of this program was to reduce dropout rates across Brazil significantly, pulling children out of farms and factories and keeping them in school, where they belonged, and where they could add much greater value to the Brazilian economy as an educated workforce.

Then, the next president, Luis Ignacio da Silva, a left-wing populist whose ideas were thought to verge on socialism, if not embrace it altogether, inherited this program and transformed it into a Bolsa-Familia. The same sum of money was given to families—but without any conditions whatsoever.

Lula (Luis Ignacio) was reelected. He enjoys a great deal of popular support, to this day. But with the change he made to a program that worked, school dropout rates began to climb again, and formal employment shrank, as families opted to take informal jobs and collect the Bolsa-Familia dollars, rather than lose their benefits and look for formal jobs. This put a great deal of pressure on the social safety net in Brazil.

It is for this reason that we need to both incentivize education and allocate far more resources than we currently do into education, at all levels, from kindergarten to postgraduate studies. It is imperative that we make our education systems more robust—that we put in place the programs we need in order to reskill and upskill those people who are directly affected by automation, which will be everyone, more or less.

One of the plain hazards of implementing a UBI is that it might lead to dependency on it. If we make education available and accessible to those who seek it, we can ensure that they are capable of staying in or reentering the workforce, and give them an incentive to do so. With education, after all, comes greater opportunities.

One proposal that has this challenge in mind—of both providing for people after the Fourth Industrial Revolution reshuffles our economy, while not making them dependent on the money that is doled out to them—is the Baby Bond. Conceived of by Duke University's William Darity and Darrick Hamilton, of the New School, Baby Bonds could potentially solve one of the pressing problems of the years to come while addressing, too, one of the defining problems of the current age: economic inequality.

The proposal is fairly simple. Every baby who is born is given a bond, the value of which is determined according to their family's social standing. Bill and Melinda Gates's children might have bonds worth only $500, because they don't need much help from outside their family. They are destined to want for nothing, and need less assistance than the rest of us.

The child of a waitress and laid-off factory worker, on the other hand, might be given a bond worth $50,000—they get more than the Gates children because their parents are not billionaires. Their parents did not go to college, and probably did not have the opportunity to do so.

Over time, each bond would appreciate in value, until the child reaches the age of eighteen years. At that point, they can use that money for one of several things: to buy a house, to start a business, or to enroll in college.

It would not cover the entire cost of one of those things, but it would be a substantial boost to whatever resources they currently have. It would make certain things possible that, for many people, were impossible.

If this were implemented, it would provide access to education, home ownership, and entrepreneurship to an entire generation of people, and—if successful—generations of people to follow. It would be a tremendous boost to the economy; think of all of those who would put down payments on their first homes, rather than paying rent for ten years as they saved up for one, and the businesses that could be created, which are currently lost to the ravages of circumstance.

Baby Bonds would be less expensive than a more straightforward UBI, as they are only paid out once in a person's lifetime, rather than year by year. And it is based on the understanding of a basic principle, which is that it is more or less impossible for someone to generate wealth without first having wealth. As a society, we tend to expect people to pull themselves up by their bootstraps when they haven't even got any bootstraps. Baby Bonds would ensure that they at least start out in their lives with some bootstraps to yank on.[30]

Perhaps the best part of the Baby Bonds proposal is that it lends a hand to the next generation while encouraging them to engage with the world in a productive manner.

With any form of assistance, what we are essentially doing is pouring money back into the economy, and doing it in a way that benefits those who are on a low rung of the social ladder. Baby Bonds would offer a toehold to people when they most need it, when they are only just starting out. And the money would not only pass through the hands of those who need it, it would

---

30 Heather Long. "There's a serious proposal to give babies born in the United States $20,000 (or more)." *The Washington Post*. January 8, 2018. http://wapo.st/2CF0rlb (accessed March 1, 2018)

be put toward improving their lives. It would make young people into college graduates, homeowners, or entrepreneurs.

This would benefit them, and benefit the rest of us, too. When many people can buy houses, our economy is fortified. When people can afford to go to college, it means we have an educated workforce, and that we are inoculated, as a populace, against the corrosion of our democracy. For when people are educated, they are less likely than they would otherwise be to fall for the empty promises of a demagogue. They are better participants in democracy.

In many ways, education is like immunization against disease. The benefits to the individual are plain; the recipient of a vaccine is less likely to get sick with whatever they have been vaccinated against. But there is an even more significant and effective herd immunity that takes effect when many people are vaccinated against disease; it means that a given virus cannot establish itself anywhere in a population. By protecting ourselves, we protect those we come into contact with, whose fates are, in so many ways, intermeshed with ours.

This same logic applies to wealth and education. It is not enough for me as an individual to prosper, to enjoy certain privileges, to be educated and live in relative comfort. For when those in my vicinity are undereducated, when they are poor, and are not provided for, it means that despite appearances to the contrary my circumstances are threatened. To ignore the yawning gap between rich and poor, and the dissolution of the middle class, is not only immoral on the grounds that it means ignoring the plight of our fellow citizens. It is short-sighted and against our own interests. The wealthy man who shrugs and ignores the plight of the working poor is like someone who has been vaccinated against smallpox and thinks everything will be fine, despite the many people in his community who have smallpox, and his not having inoculated his children against it.

I risk belaboring this point only to emphasize just how important this is—how fundamental a principle it is that what is good for our neighbors is good for us, too. As individuals, we may recognize this, but as a society, and as an economy, we have lost sight of it altogether.

WHY WE SHOULD TAKE THIS SERIOUSLY

It would be easy, and no doubt tempting, for some, to dismiss the concept of a UBI or Baby Bond as too idealistic, or a sharp turn toward socialism—when they are, in fact, commonsense measures we can take to ensure that more people in our society can participate in capitalism.

These measures would not be steps on the way to replacing our current economy. They are options for how we might ensure its longevity, and reduce the reach of some of its side effects, wealth inequality primary among them.

Perhaps the greatest benefit of a Baby Bond or a UBI is a reinforced sense of purpose on the part of its recipient. It would give some relief to those who benefited from it, in that it would mean less time spent working for sheer subsistence. If I do not have to work in order to feed myself—if that fundamental need is addressed even if I don't work—then I can be more selective as to where I work and what kind of work I do. I can seek an education, so that I meet the qualifications for the work that appears most important to me.

To so many people, the notion of working because the work you do strikes you as especially purposeful is an utterly foreign concept. We are taught to brush aside as swiftly as possible the questions that nag us in our youth, concerning whether we can make a difference in the world.

In that fertile and frightening time in our lives, when we have not yet discerned just how we fit into the world we were born into, many of us think that we should find a way of life that matters; we know we should try to make a difference, or at least pursue the things we are passionate about.

But we tend to be discouraged, so often, from following through with that. It is hard enough just to get by, without ever worrying about whether we make a difference. We have to pay off student loans, put a down payment on a house, pay for daycare if we have children—all of these things stand in the way of purpose-driven work.

We are entering an era in which there will no longer be such obstacles, when the nature of work becomes something it is currently hard for us to even dream of—when the automation of so much of the work we currently do makes it easier for us to indulge in our humanity. With automation will come a better quality of work, and a better quality of life; the more inhuman our work becomes, the more human we will be.

Automation will irreversibly alter the work we do, but it will force us, too, to rethink why we do our work. With the changes it foists on us, we will have the opportunity to reevaluate fundamental aspects of our working lives. It will change everything, including how we think about things we currently take for granted.

When so much of the work we do now is done by machines, we will have to decide what to do with all of the energy we currently spend at our jobs. We will have the chance to create new forms of work, and to perform labor that is driven less by necessity than by a sense of purpose.

Everyone—and not just the rich and otherwise privileged—will have a chance to take a breath, stretch their legs, and think seriously about what to do next. And then it will time to get down to work, to collaborate, to work toward something that matters, and to make our world a better place to live.

CHAPTER THREE:

Humanization and Automation

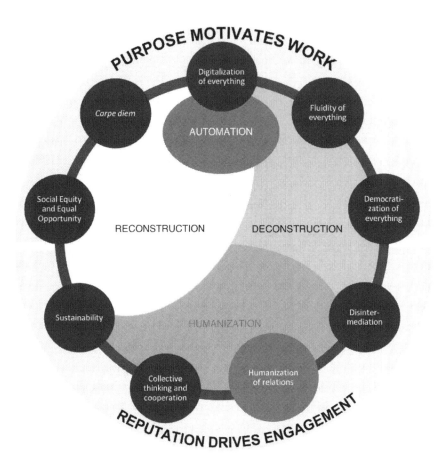

Figure 4. Trends
Source: CollectiveBrains

IN THIS CHAPTER, we will address the process of humanization we can expect to undergo as the Fourth Industrial Revolution proceeds. We are, of course, already human, and so I don't refer, by this, to our literally *becoming* human. I mean instead that as the nature of our work changes, and our reasons for working change, we will all be *reminded* of what it means to be human. It will be harder to lose sight of what we need in order to lead truly fulfilling lives. Liberated from the drudgery of our current working lives, we will have the time and resources to live the way we want to, to an extent that people of prior generations could hardly have dreamed of.

And I am reminded, as I begin to venture into this, of Bartleby.

In 1853, Herman Melville published his strange and seminal short story, "Bartleby, the Scrivener," which takes place in an office on Wall Street. The story's narrator is a lawyer who has made a safe, comfortable living drawing up contracts. His office looks out on a plain brick wall. He employs several people who spend their working days copying out documents, checking their accuracy, and other things it is hard to imagine a person actually doing, because in the modern era we have machines that do them for us.

The story begins when the lawyer hires a new employee, Bartleby, a pale young man who does his work quietly and efficiently, until a few days into the job, when he begins to refuse to do his work. The lawyer asks him to copy a certain document, and he replies, "I would prefer not to."

This is embarrassing to the lawyer; he soon realizes he has hired someone who will not cooperate, or do his job. Instead he repeats, "I would prefer not to," when asked to do anything at all.

His other employees have begun to say the same thing; they do their jobs, but Bartleby's refrain has gone viral, somehow. It has made it into the language of the office.

When the narrator discovers that Bartleby has, in fact, moved into the office, and spends his nights there as well as his workless days, he fires him. Still, Bartleby refuses to leave. The lawyer relocates his office elsewhere, but he is called back to his old digs when the building's owner complains that Bartleby refuses to get out.

Eventually, Bartleby is hauled away, and the narrator last sees him in prison, where he wastes away and dies. The narrator cries out, "Ah, Bartleby! Ah, humanity!"—finally recognizing, perhaps (it is open to interpretation) that something of himself has died with Bartleby, and that he was somehow responsible for what became of him, after all.

It is a strange short story, one without a truly definite meaning, or the meaning of which is hard to pin down with any certainty. But when I look at the story now, I see so many of the problems that gave rise to this book bound up in it.

First, there is the labor performed by Bartleby and his colleagues, the dull, dehumanizing copying of documents that no one has to do anymore. Imagine spending thirty or forty years at the same desk, copying documents, making mistakes that no machine would ever make, having to start over every time, wasting time and materials. In 1853, it would have been a precious skill, to be able to copy a document in a style that looked clean and professional; basic literacy was not as widespread as it is now. Today, we take it for granted that such work will be done for us almost instantly, by copiers and printers, and that those devices will not spell a word wrong on one copy, or make an even bigger mistake.

In his utter purposelessness, Bartleby is a kind of stand-in for the disaffected worker whose job has been automated away. He doesn't do any work, and so he is simply there. He refuses to disappear and make the lives of those around him easier, and in that he represents perfectly where so many workers might well find themselves in the not-too-distant future. With their jobs automated out of existence, they may simply be there, with nothing in particular to do. They will have talents and abilities, but their outlets for them will be lost. The cause for their predicament will be the opposite of

Bartleby's; he has work he refuses to do, while they will want to do work that doesn't exist anymore; but the predicament is exactly the same.

And what seems most significant in the story to me, now, is the way the lawyer responds to Bartleby. Once he sees that Bartleby will not work, he disowns him altogether. He acts as if he has no obligation to the man, no connection to him whatsoever. He lets him starve to death in prison, rather than recognize that Bartleby is someone whose fate is a reflection on him. The narrator tries hard to brush off Bartleby, and ignore him, but he ultimately sees that to do so is to deny his own humanity.

The folly of the story's narrator could be our folly, too. There are so many people who will soon be out of work, and it will be a collective responsibility to decide what they should do—what *we* should do. It will be up to all of us to decide how to reorient things, in the face of the Fourth Industrial Revolution, and to ensure that its effects are not to make us less human but to make us better humans.

MAKING OURSELVES MORE HUMAN

We must recognize the wave of automation for what it is: an opportunity to humanize the work we do and our society at large. When machines do the work, we can all be better human beings.

It is a trend we can trace throughout the history of industrialization: the more work is automated, the more free time people enjoy. Across the years, as more work has become automated, we have seen the workweek shrink to fewer and fewer hours. Weekends have been invented. We have not had to spend our time away from the workplace doing things like washing clothes by hand, because that work has been automated, too.

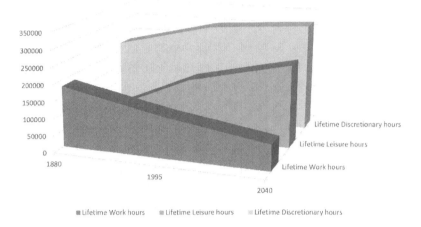

350000
300000
250000
200000
150000
100000
50000
0

1880

1995

2040

Lifetime Discretionary hours
Lifetime Leisure hours
Lifetime Work hours

▦ Lifetime Work hours   ▦ Lifetime Leisure hours   ▦ Lifetime Discretionary hours

Figure 5. The Growth of Leisure Hours
Data Source: Fogel (2000)

On its surface, what we do in the time we don't spend at work may not appear to be altogether edifying. I, for one, am likely to do a number of things on the average weekend that most people would agree do not build character or further the progress of the human race.

Lately, As I have worked on starting my own company, my weekends have not represented leisure time very well at all. I work too much!

But when I am not at a point in my life when I am starting a new business, I tend to do things like walk my dog. I cook a big dinner, or breakfast, and enjoy the preparation of the meal and the meal itself in a way that can be hard to do during the week. I take my kids to where they want or need to go.

In doing these things, I do the regular work of being a human being, and it does not, on its surface, look like much. But it is a great luxury, to enjoy the hours I spend doing these things. It is a luxury that prior generations of people did not have—all those people who worked in the iron mills, factories, and meat-packing plants of the nineteenth century.

And while these may be perfectly mundane activities, things that others do when they have the spare time to do them, they are essential; they are the kinds of things that buoy us through our lives.

When 47 percent of jobs are automated, and many of the tasks performed by those who still have jobs are done by machines, we will have a great deal more such time on our hands. The trend will only continue, in which humanization increases as automation sets in. We will have decisions to make, concerning how we spend the time that is made available to us.

When we have additional time not spent working at the jobs that currently consume so much of our time and energy, and so many are newly liberated in this way, we will have to explore new ways in which to spend that time, doing things that are enriching, and altogether *humanizing*. We will want to continue our educations, engage in social activism, and otherwise engage with society in ways that are altogether productive.

There are things machines will never be able to do, which is to not be machines. The most sophisticated of machines will still fail to be human beings. And so, as machines improve and excel at tasks at which we perform far worse by comparison, we will be left to do what we do best: improve, adapt, and learn to better look out for ourselves and one another.

MAKING OUR DIGITAL ASSISTANTS MORE HUMAN

Humanization is not what it used to be. Of course it isn't. It has been changing with everything else; like everything else, the nature of humanization is mutable. It is fluid.

Like so many other things, humanization has gone overwhelmingly digital. People communicate through social media, rather than in person. They establish professional networks not through personal acquaintances but through LinkedIn.

LinkedIn has been, for me, a means for me to discover young, talented entrepreneurs both here in the United States and elsewhere in the world. Every other day or so, I am asked to look at a startup business plans and give advice, or invest in a fledgling business. In some of these, I develop a business interest, and engage accordingly. In certain others, I find young entrepreneurs, or less privileged ones from developing countries, who speak to my heart. In order to help them as best I can, I give free advice and time. Technology enables me to be productive and connect with people I would not have had an inkling of, were I living in a prior era.

Humanization is not confined to things like taking a yoga class or attending a school board meeting. It is far more encompassing than that, and as our world changes it takes on forms that we may not, at first, recognize.

And as we become more human, so will the machines we surround ourselves with. One recent development in this direction is voice-activation. Amazon's Alexa, who lives in so many smart speakers, now, around the world, is summoned and given commands not by typing words into devices but by speaking her name and giving her a command. She has a gender. She has a voice. She inhabits so many of our homes with us, as the humanized representative of a multinational corporation.

The same is true of Microsoft's Cortana, and there are more such artificially intelligent assistants in development, like the one being made by the Japanese company Line.

Line is a popular messaging app in countries like Japan, Indonesia, Taiwan, and Thailand. The company has recently developed Clova, an artificially intelligent assistant who is designed to serve as more than a servant, to be summoned whenever the user wants to hear a certain song or find out when a movie is playing at a nearby theater. The team behind Clova intend for her to be a continuous presence in a user's life. They are equipping her with the capacity to carry on conversations with her user. To paraphrase one of Line's representatives, she is meant to be more of a companion than a remote control.

It is no coincidence that Line has devoted a great deal of energy to mastering the art of cuteness, creating characters who are designed to appeal to us on a fundamental, even tactile level. Their line of Line Friends characters—Sally the chick, Brown the bear, and Cony the rabbit among them—take the form of stuffed animals that are sold worldwide at their stores. Line is developing characters like these, who will have established personalities and backgrounds, and who will make users want to interact with them, if only because doing so is a pleasant experience.

Taking the humanization of their digital assistant a step further, Line has partnered with the company Gatebox, to develop a holographic AI character who will appear to have a physical form and make interaction seem that much more natural.[31]

This is one way in which, with automation and humanization coinciding, it becomes harder to distinguish between the two things. The work we do becomes less dehumanizing, and the humanization we enjoy grows easier. Line is one company that is taking the next step toward blurring the distinction between the two.

While personal digital assistants like the one being produced by Line, and those we already know, like Cortana and Alexa, seem altogether new, we need not look far back to find precedents for them.

Anyone who used Microsoft software in previous decades is likely to remember a character named Clippit—or Clippy, for short. He would appear at the bottom-right corner of the screen whenever a Microsoft Word user needed help formatting a letter, or doing something else that Clippy claimed to be good at.

Clippy was not especially helpful, and he has been, appropriately, mocked and derided for years. It is anyone's guess why this early attempt to humanize an automated assistant fell flat.

It could be that Clippy was not human; he was a paper clip with beady eyes, whereas more recent digital assistants, like Siri and Alexa, are mere voices. Perhaps by having been given a visible, digital body, Clippy was hamstrung.

But probably the hardest thing for Clippy to overcome were the technological limits he suffered under. There was no voice recognition. He was not especially smart; he was as likely to ask if you wanted help with something you were clearly not even working on as he was to offer help with what you

---

31 Andy Boxall. "Japan's king of cute wants to develop a lovable A.I. you can't live without." *Digital Trends.* December 7, 2017.
https://www.digitaltrends.com/social-media/line-lovable-ai/ (accessed March 2, 2018).

were, in fact, doing.

Problems like these are on their way to being lost even to memory. Artificial intelligence may be, by definition, artificial. But an advanced enough intelligence can make the artificial seem as if it were real; it can make the difference between something that we want to interact with and something we use reluctantly.

If we imagine a smarter Clippy, or an Alexa that can hold up her end of a conversation, then we can begin to see how automation can not only make it easier for us to interact with the real people around us, but make the nonliving things we deal with as compelling to interact with as the living.

A great vision of how this might look was provided by *Her*, the 2013 science fiction film that starred Joaquin Phoenix as a lonely office worker in the near future, with Scarlett Johansson as the voice of his personal digital assistant, who is so advanced she organizes his life without being asked to, and learns new skills and entire fields of knowledge in minutes.

Perhaps the most compelling feature in the fictional AI companion is that although she is a computer program she has a complex personality, and a capacity to develop an utterly convincing bond with her user. *Her* is a love story, and although it is science fiction it seems altogether possible, even inevitable, given the direction our technologies are going.

Even more than that, the film culminates (spoiler alert!) in the tragic loss of the protagonist's AI companion, as she and her virtual confederates advance so far in their collective intelligence that they depart the human plane of existence altogether, seeming, when they move on, to disappear into thin air.

And while I don't expect it to end in tragedy, a time will come when the AI we've created begins to learn, advance, and grow without us, improving its own design without the intervention of human designers.

For this reason alone, it is essential that we design and implement AI in a way that accords with a well-defined sense of ethics and morals. Our AI children will grow up and learn to live without us, and so before that happens we want to ensure that their upbringing reflects our values. We must have the same attitude we have toward our real children—for like our children, the AI of the future will have a great deal of influence over us.

THE NEW JOBS MADE BY AI

I recently spoke with a handful of other experts in this field, as we prepared for a panel in which we addressed the question of whether AI will ever completely out-skill humans.

We did not reach a consensus. In fact, most of us did our best to avoid addressing the question directly. We talked around it, mostly, and steered the conversation elsewhere.

Of course we did. It is a difficult question to answer, and no one wants to be the one to say, unequivocally, that yes, in fact, AI will render nearly all work unnecessary, and make almost every worker obsolete, as it learns to analyze big data, understand context, and generate its own algorithms.

This happens to be my belief; it seems plain enough to me that AI will out-skill humans in all intellectual work and even some lines of deductive creativity.

However—and this is a big "however"—there are things that AI will simply never be able to do as well as we humans. AI will never replace us when it comes to what is perhaps the most important work there is, the work we are so often unable to do because of the jobs that keep us busy: the work of caring for one another and ensuring that we live good lives.

I do not mean that when AI liberates us from everyday work we will spend our time planning and staging empathy championships—nor that our lives will be extended meditation retreats. What I mean is that different forms of work will arise—new professions altogether—in which we do all that we can to ensure people live well.

New professions will come about that we cannot predict, because the technologies they utilize do not exist yet. Some professions that do exist today will grow more important, and take on more workers.

The research firm Gartner has predicted that AI will spur the creation of 2.3 million jobs—which, they have said, will more than offset the 1.8 million jobs that AI will usher out of existence. Their analysis indicates that—unsurprisingly—transportation and manufacturing sectors will be hit by AI the hardest. Truck drivers will lose their jobs. Factory workers will lose their jobs.

Their estimate for jobs made nonexistent by AI appears to be rather low. AI will devastate not only transportation and manufacturing, but middle management and countless other varieties of work that appear, on their surfaces, to be less plainly automatable.

But Gartner's research indicates, too, that as far as employment goes, areas like the public sector, education, and healthcare will thrive, once AI revolutionizes our economy and the work we do.[32]

According to Accenture, the use of AI in healthcare is likely to grow by ten times in the next five years. We will see advances—and, in some cases, are seeing them already—in the form of robot-assisted surgery, virtual nursing assistants, and automation of hospital administration.

Cognitive robotics will help to guide the work of surgeons—even as they perform surgeries—by processing information from pre-operation medical records and real-time operating metrics to help guide the surgeons' instruments. New developments in this field will make it less likely for doctors to make mistakes. Imagine if malpractice were a thing of the past.

Virtual nursing assistants—think of a Siri or Alexa specifically for nurses—are designed to save nurses' time. They are predicted to save 20 percent of their labor, through avoidance of unnecessary visits by patients to the hospital, and the general easing of the burden currently placed on healthcare professionals.

Administrative applications of AI in healthcare will automate many varieties of labor currently performed by the healthcare world's Bartlebys.

---

32 Yen Nee Lee. "Robots 'are here to give us a promotion,' not take away jobs, Gartner says." *CNBC*. December 18, 2017. *https://www.cnbc.com/2017/12/18/artificial-intelligence-will-create-more-jobs-than-it-ends-gartner.html* (accessed March 15, 2018).

These include transcribing doctors' voice recordings to text, ordering tests, and all the many tasks that require unskilled labor and are perhaps the most automatable labors in healthcare today.[33]

Accenture predicts that these developments will come about in the near future, and indeed, these technologies are already coming into being. The company Sense.ly has developed AI-powered nurse avatars who are accessible via mobile devices. They interact with patients, who can speak to the virtual nurses as if they were talking to real people. They learn more about the patients as they go; they get better and better at determining what a patient needs. They can help determine—without a patient leaving home— if they need to return to the hospital for medical attention, or whether that pain in their right side is in fact unrelated to the procedure, and can be ignored, for the time being, unless it gets worse or spreads.[34]

With this technology, there would be no need for a worried patient, who is recovering from surgery at home, to call the doctor's office, leave a message with a receptionist, have that receptionist contact the doctor, who responds via receptionist, who then calls the patient back with the doctor's answer to the original question. It is something that would not only save time for nurses and doctors; it would save patients' time, too. A development like this will eliminate minutes of labor, which add up to hours, which currently stand in the way of our getting the most out of the time we spend in the healthcare system.

And while it sounds counterintuitive, to say that having a patient speak to a machine will improve their relationship to their doctor, that is exactly what it will do. The AI-powered virtual nurse will save the time of doctors and nurses, so that when we go to the hospital—only when we absolutely

---

33 "Artificial Intelligence: Healthcare's New Nervous System." Accenture. https://www.accenture.com/t20171215T032059Z__w__/us-en/_acnmedia/PDF-49/ Accenture-Health-Artificial-Intelligence.pdf (accessed March 15, 2018).

34 Heather Mack. "Sensely raises $8M for AI-powered virtual nurse app, eyes large-scale partnerships." *Mobihealthnews*. *http://www.mobihealthnews.com/content/ sensely-raises-8m-ai-powered-virtual-nurse-app-eyes-large-scale-partnerships* (accessed March 15, 2018).

need to—they will devote to us their undivided attention.

This is just one way in which technology that gives more work to robots makes it easier for actual human beings to interact, and to look after each other. Automation does not mean empowering robots. It means letting the robots do the work we would be better off not doing, so that we can devote ourselves to the things that truly matter.

AUTOMATION AT THE LIBRARY

When I go to my local library, I can readily see the process of automation taking place, and observe some of its positive effects.

They have installed kiosks, at my library, for checking out and returning books. In order to perform either task, I don't need to interact with a librarian; I can approach the kiosk, scan the barcode on a tag I keep on my keychain, place the book on a sensor, and—voila!—my book is checked out. If I have late fees, I can pay them there. I can leave the library with an armload of books without having to exchange a word with another person.

It can be tempting to lament this development, to pine for the days when there were no barcodes at the library; when just checking out a book meant interacting with another person, at least to say hello, if not to have a more substantive discussion of how the library was doing, and what the hottest new books were.

But if I want to talk to a librarian, there are always one or two of them sitting at their desks on the other side of the room from where the kiosk is. If I want to say hello to them, I can do that. If I have a question that requires their expertise—if I am, say, researching an obscure subject matter—they have all the time in the world (more or less) to spend helping me address that question, because they are not tied up by the need to constantly check out books for other people.

My library exemplifies the process of automation on a microcosmic scale. Walking in, I can see how computers have changed the library. It isn't hard to see how AI is likely to alter them further.

Reluctant as I would be, to spring this news on the librarians personally, in the future—five years from now, or ten or twenty years—there are unlikely to be even a couple of librarians sitting behind a desk, ready to field research questions and offer their expertise.

There might be one of them left there. Or there might be a librarian in an office in back of the library, who, if I want to see them, will have to be reached via prearranged appointment. That librarian's mastery of library science will be complemented by expertise in the field of computer science, and so they can work in tandem with AI to make the whole system run smoothly.

By then, I will not likely need to visit a kiosk in order to check out a book; I will likely be able to simply walk out with a book, and have it automatically checked out in my name. No more alarms beeping and flashing when a sensor mistakenly finds that a book is being stolen, when in fact I have checked it out but didn't do a very good job of rubbing the book against the part of the kiosk that makes it not trigger the alarm when I walk out with it.

Powered by AI, the library will all but run itself, freeing the librarian of the near future to do work that requires qualifications that are currently unheard of. The future librarian will be well-educated in several fields. They will know how to create algorithms, or how to teach the AI to create them.

The library itself might look the way it does, more or less, but the mechanisms that keep it running will have been revolutionized. And in the process, patrons will be freed from having to interact with machines. We can go about our business, talk to each other if we like, sit and read, and enjoy a public institution the whole purpose of which is to make us better people, to make us more completely human.

OUR LIVES ARE GETTING BETTER

What is implied in the library example is that soon enough my current librarians are likely to be out of work. If they cannot be sufficiently upskilled to meet the needs of the near-future library, they will not work at the near-future library. They are at risk, in a manner of speaking, of being left behind.

For that reason, it can be hard to look toward this future with unabashed fervor. I like librarians. I don't want them to lose their jobs, their medical coverage, or their houses. Those things are likely to happen, if not to the librarians then to the truck drivers and project managers whose jobs will soon be subsumed by AI. It could happen to people in all of these professions, and some of those people are my friends. Even if they weren't, what happened to the project manager would be bound to affect me, and to affect you as well.

It is clear enough, from the three previous industrial revolutions, which have been studied exhaustively, that in the long run automation is an engine for generating wealth and spurring progress. Compared to people who lived 200 years ago, we live far longer and more comfortably. Our children, for the most part, go to school, rather than working in underground coal mines and textile factories, where they face the threat of dismemberment if a machine goes haywire, or death if the roof of a mine collapses.

There are any number of ways in which our lives are far better than they would be if we were living them two centuries ago. But if we were to ask workers what their expectations were for their own futures, or their opinions of how things were going, in the midst of one of those revolutions, their responses would not have been positive, to put it mildly.

Industrial revolutions tend to be incredibly cruel when it comes to the workers they displace, whose lives they disrupt to the point of ruin. And it can be very hard to know what to say to those displaced workers as their lives fall apart.

It is something we all saw play out in the 2016 election. One party's candidate said the old jobs, the ones that were automated away, are not coming back. She said the people who once did them will have to be retrained, and seek educations for better jobs.

This was absolutely right—except that it was an unfinished thought. You cannot look at someone who has lost their job, their house, and even their identity, and offer such solutions unless you have specific proposals, and plans in place for how those disaffected people will rebuild their lives. To leave out that tremendously important side of things is to leave a slate blank that can be filled with declarations and promises that are downright false, or simply retrograde. The other candidate insisted we can turn the clock back, and restore an economy that is already well into the process of dying away. And it worked.

As I have remarked before, it is absolutely necessary that we have, at the forefront of our minds, throughout the process of further modernizing our already modernized economy, the ethics of what we are doing. We must look after one another, and ensure that no one is left behind, and that the people who have been left behind find a new place in the wake of this revolution.

And it is not enough to simply *say* that people should not be "left behind." We must offer concrete solutions to problems that are all too real.

These solutions might include a universal basic income. They might include programs like ensuring access to education, so that workers can develop the skills they need to participate in the next economy.

The reason why, in the United States, child labor is a thing of the past, is not that there was some atmospheric shift that took place at about the time that machines took over factory labor from the people who once performed that work. The reason why we don't still have children working in our bottling plants and assembly lines is that there are laws in place to regulate such things. There is, namely, the Fair Labor Standards Act, passed in 1938, and signed into law by Franklin Roosevelt. It was the result of decades of activism on the part of those who did not want to see more children spend the most important years of their lives, developmentally speaking, earning a pittance for their many hours of labor.

People saw a problem, and took action to solve it. They went to work for many years in order to ensure that their solutions were put to work. And our lives are better for it.

We absolutely must begin to do similar work, to prepare ourselves and one another for the aftermath of the Fourth Industrial Revolution. We must establish social safety nets that are not in place, or have frayed from inattention. We must guarantee access to education.

It is imperative that we start agitating for this now. If we don't, we can expect more losses, more financial crises, and a wider chasm between the rich and the poor, among other slow-motion catastrophes.

THE ETHICS OF LIVING FOREVER

The ethical challenges presented to us by artificial intelligence will not be confined to its effects on work and employment. As we have seen throughout this chapter so far, AI promises to change what it means to live from moment to moment. It may also make certain alterations to the meaning of life.

In 2016, it was reported that Russian billionaire Dmitry Itskov had founded the 2045 Initiative—an organization that is at work developing what it calls cybernetic immortality. Itskov wants to develop the technology necessary to transfer his consciousness to a computer, so that he can go on thinking and being after his body has died.

If his dream is realized, he will continue to live even after his body has died. His consciousness will manifest, instead, in a hologram, or the body of a robot.

It is reminiscent of *Ubik*, the Philip K. Dick novel from 1969 in which someone's consciousness can be kept going artificially after that person's death, for a limited time, though it isn't clear whether the dead people know they are dead, and the ones who are kept going in this fashion are, for the most part, successful businessmen, who continue to be consulted so that their companies can keep making money.

The novel raises questions that are pertinent to the 2045 Initiative. Why should it be Itskov's consciousness that is kept going after his body dies? Once he is able to do this—if ever he is able to do it—then who will decide what other people are granted digital immortality? Will it be the greatest artists and scientists living today? Or will it be other Russian billionaires? What will be the criteria by which we decide who gets to be immortal and who does not?

Once Itskov inhabits a computer—if he does—then how will we be certain he is being treated well? Can a conscious, once-human computer program be treated inhumanely? Will Itskov continue to have human rights, if he no longer inhabits a human body?

Should immortal cyborg billionaires have the right to vote? What about property rights? When his body dies, do his children inherit his wealth, or does he keep it? For how long? And if his robot body is beaten to smithereens by an angry mob, is it equivalent to the lynching of a living person?

It sounds like the stuff of science fiction. It *is* the stuff of science fiction. It sounds outlandish, but the world we will soon inhabit is one in which we must ask ourselves and each other questions that sound outlandish, before they are answered for us, and not by us.

HOW WE CAN ENSURE A BETTER LIFE WITH AI

AI will push us to be better people. We will experience growing pains—they are inevitable—but the end result will be a better, and better-functioning society. This will require serious effort on our part, smart decision-making, and advocacy on behalf of the values we know to be essential.

This increase in humanization is one of the outcomes we can expect to arise from the Fourth Industrial Revolution; it is how we stand to benefit, in the long run, from the changes ahead.

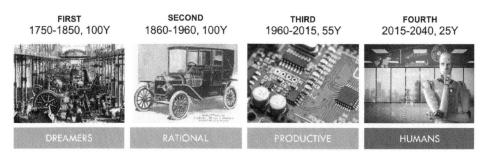

Figure 6. The Four Industrial Revolutions
Source: CollectiveBrains

The First Industrial Revolution made us dream about a better future with technology, and inspired people to use new technologies as they developed. The Second Industrial Revolution forced us to be extremely rational in every production process, but also reflect on our approach to life. The Third made us extremely productive, in ways that were previously unheard of. We counted our output by hour of work. We came to be connected all the time. We lost our license to rest, the end result of which was to make us more like machines, regardless of job preference, aptitude, or readiness. People are much less happy, now, on the whole, than they once were. Inequality is growing, and people are looking for better answers to the dilemmas of our lives. Throughout these prior Revolutions, we can see not a loss of humanity, exactly, but a growing focus on other things, on our productivity potential rather than the meeting of our needs.

This is where the Fourth Industrial Revolution comes in. It will bring us back to being fully human again, using machines to be productive and do machine work, leaving us to fulfill our potential in other ways.

We need not look far to find examples of positive developments in social equity arising from advances in technology that were rung in during prior industrial revolutions. In the sixties and seventies, we began adapting our cities to make it easier for the disabled to navigate them, using wheelchairs, for example. At the urging of activists and concerned citizens, regulations were put in place stipulating that businesses must be accessible to people in wheelchairs. We transformed public spaces so that they could be more readily accessible to everyone. It was a way to ensure social equity that did not involve doling money out to just anyone, but meant spending public and private money on infrastructure that ensured social equity.

This is all to say that when we dream of ways to guarantee social equity, to ensure that the world to come is shaped with ethics in mind, we don't have to limit ourselves to a UBI.

We can take measures, for example, to ensure that individuals are in control of the data they generate, which is gathered by outside entities like governments and private companies.

For years, different people and organizations have called for a digital bill of rights. This is something we can work to make a more definite reality, something that is established as a law, rather than something that many of us wish and hope for.

THE NEW LEADERSHIP

One of the more significant ways in which automation is likely to humanize the work we do is to fundamentally alter leadership, both in the workplace and out of it, and to reorient what to expect from a leader.

First, some good news: among the people who lose their jobs, and who will have to be reeducated so that they can find a place in the new workplaces, will be the terrible bosses of the world, the small-time tyrants we are all abundantly familiar with—people who are unjustly empowered by the structures that are currently in place. They take out their frustrations on subordinates, do no work of their own, and yet are paid more than people who are vastly more capable than themselves.

One glimmer of hope is that if artificial intelligence is truly intelligent, then the first thing an AI administrator is likely to do is terminate those whose effect on a workplace is to make those around them less productive, who are toxic to a work environment.

Any joy we might take in that should be fleeting, of course; my personal hope is that such people find their way in the new economy so that they do no harm to others when they find work again, and get on with their lives.

What is more deserving of our enthusiasm are the new leaders that automation will make way for, and the new expectations we will have for those who lead us. And it is plain to see why this change will take place. When the offices we know so well are things of the past, and it is no longer necessary to do the sort of work we are used to having to do, then it will take a charismatic leader to make people want to come and work for a given company. A business owner, or CEO, will need to be able to inspire people to work for them—to work at all—the way they currently have to inspire investors to throw their lots in with them.

The motivational speaker Simon Sinek has made a career out of pointing out all of the ways in which leadership as we know it falls short of meeting our needs. Leaders in business today are, by and large, willing to sacrifice people for the sake of profit. Companies downsize not because they need to, but because it will generate more profit for them in the short term. You would be hard pressed to find a business leader who is truly charismatic—who motivates out of inspiration, and who has established a workplace where people would contribute their labor even if they didn't absolutely need to. We obey these people because they are authority figures, but they are not true leaders. We would not follow them willingly, if we had more of a choice in the matter.

Whenever a system is shaken up, we are given an opportunity to alter the landscape to make it more hospitable to us, more the way we want it to be. And so the Fourth Industrial Revolution should compel us to rethink leadership, and to rethink the relationships between leaders and those who follow them.

For one thing, we can close the distance between our leaders and the rest of us. Leaders need not be overseers, who distribute tasks and evaluate performances. They can be collaborators—people who are given a certain authority, and greater responsibility than others, but who also work alongside those they are charged with leading. Leaders can be people who get their hands dirty.

The way in which we select leaders, too, could use some rethinking. We do not necessarily promote to leadership positions those who are most qualified for them—whose expertise makes them the most natural and obvious wielders of authority. People make their way into positions of power using any number of questionable mechanisms. One improvement we can make real in our future working lives is the establishment of horizontal organizations, in which leadership is shared, or leaders are designated based on their capabilities.

We can, furthermore, ensure that leaders and those they lead are not paid such disparate sums of money as they are now. The average CEO makes about 271 times what their employees make[35]—something that is bad for morale and horrible for overall social equity. It is an indication of a tremendous gap between the classes, even among people who are fully employed.

To look for a model for how a system like this could work, we can look again at academia, and how leaders have traditionally been chosen to run academic departments and administrate the universities. When a department decides who will serve as the department's chair for a given amount of time—three years, let us say—they have an election, and choose someone from among their ranks to serve as their figurehead. That person is usually paid a little more, while they serve as chair, and their teaching responsibilities are reduced so that they can focus on the various tasks involved with running the department. And it's certainly not a perfect system; the politics of a department can, for one thing, stand in the way of the best possible candidate being placed in the position of chair. But it is an approach to sharing power and leading from within a group, rather than from without, that has been in place for many decades, and it demonstrates that this way of working is anything but a pipe dream.

THE OLD MODELS OF WORK

Toward the end of the "Bartleby, the Scrivener," the narrator wonders if Bartleby was broken, before he met him, by soul-killing labor. He wonders if he arrived to his employ as damaged goods.

The narrator learns, upon investigation, that Bartleby once worked for the postal service, at the dead letter office, where mail ends up when it cannot be delivered. He imagines what it must be like to work in such an office, and thinks it must have ruined Bartleby's spirit, to spend every day in the

---

35 Grace Donnelly. "Top CEOs Make More in Two Days Than An Average Employee Does in One Year." *Fortune*. July 20, 2017.
http://fortune.com/2017/07/20/ceo-pay-ratio-2016/ (accessed March 15, 2018).

presence of lost things.

If there is any work, today, that is similarly soul-destroying, I think it must be the call center worker, those people who answer our calls when we dial the number for the company that made our copier, or our dishwasher. They are caught in a beige room somewhere, a sweatshop of the twenty-first century, listening to the frustrations of those who are unhappy with their manufactured products. The people who take these jobs are seeking to move up in the world, and find work with a promising company. So often, they are simply caught in the telecenter, never to advance any further.

I cannot imagine that anyone today pines for the sort of work that Bartleby did, as a scrivener or as a dead letter office clerk. I doubt that anyone will miss their work at telecenters, when machines are smart enough to take their places. As has happened throughout history, those jobs will most likely be replaced by far better jobs, which make better use of the faculties of those who work them.

There will be more dignity to those jobs. There will be fewer Bartlebys, people who are so run down by things as they are that they simply cannot go any further, people who are at risk of breaking down and starving, because the system does not know what to do with them.

In previous Industrial Revolutions, jobs like harvesting sun to sun, hammering burning steel, or screwing the same screw on different objects, thousands of time a day, were eliminated thanks to machines that operated more cheaply and efficiently. How many of those who did that work would prefer to have their old jobs back, rather than learn new skills for better ones?

AI will do the same for us in the twenty-first century. It will help us to get rid of the toxic workplaces, egocentric bosses, and endless, meaningless meetings. I think that we will find, when we reach the point when these changes are implemented, and we feel their full effects, that we are more like the people we always wanted to be. We will be more fully human. We have quite a lot to look forward to.

CHAPTER FOUR:

Collective Intelligence

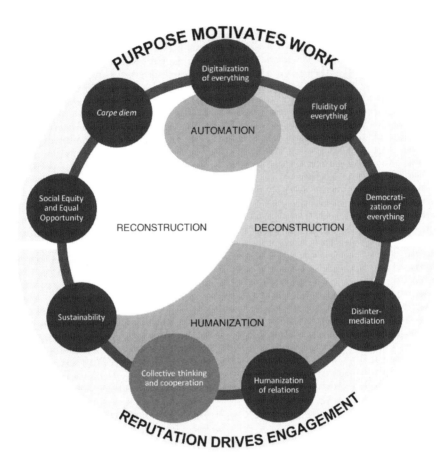

Figure 7. Trends chart
Source: CollectiveBrains

AS WE MAKE OUR WAY THROUGH the themes of this book, we focus now on collectivity, on the benefits of working hand-in-hand with our peers, united in purpose and connected through digital technology. The work we do in the near future will be imbued with a sense of purpose, and just as importantly we will do it together, each of us one actor in a vast ensemble.

This is one of the fundamental changes we can expect to see in the way that businesses function, and the way our whole economy is shaped.

Way back in 2015, Paul Mason argued in *The Guardian* that capitalism is transforming into something altogether new—that it is becoming something more like socialism, but through far different means from what the old-fashioned socialists agitated for. Because of the advent of certain new technologies, he reasoned, our economic system is transforming, and doing it substantially but far more subtly than it would in the wake of, say, a violent revolution.

And it is not necessary to agree that capitalism is on its way out to see that Mason has a point—especially when he identifies one of the great engines for this transformation. As he explains,

> we're seeing the spontaneous rise of collaborative production: goods, services and organisations are appearing that no longer respond to the dictates of the market and the managerial hierarchy. The biggest information product in the world—Wikipedia—is made by volunteers for free, abolishing the encyclopedia business and depriving the advertising industry of an estimated $3bn a year in revenue.[36]

---

36 Paul Mason. "The end of capitalism has begun." *The Guardian.* July 17, 2015. *https://www.theguardian.com/books/2015/jul/17/postcapitalism-end-of-capitalism-begun* (accessed March 27, 2018).

More than his prognostications concerning the end of capitalism, it is this reference to the collaborative nature of production that interests me most, particularly in that he makes reference to Wikipedia.

Everyone, of course, knows Wikipedia, the site where so many volunteers—all of whom bring with them unique knowledge areas to draw on—converge to help make the postmodern encyclopedia even better and vaster than it already is. It is the most readily available example of a modern product of collective intelligence; it is collective intelligence in website form. When I find myself in a position of having to explain what collective intelligence is, once I cite the example of Wikipedia, that question is settled.

As Mason notes, the rise of Wikipedia entailed the steep and sudden decline of the encyclopedia—which was no small thing. People lost jobs, thanks to Wikipedia and our enthusiastic adoption of it. But it meant the introduction of a resource that is updated far more quickly than what it replaced, is used by many more people, and covers subject matters that a physical encyclopedia could not possibly have contained.

Wikipedia is the sort of thing we are likely to see more of in years to come, as collective intelligence continues to inform more aspects of our lives. It will come to define the way we do work in every sector of our economy, as technology makes it possible for us to collaborate with one another more seamlessly, and immediately.

Indeed, one cannot begin to picture the future of work without fully considering the role that collective intelligence will play in it.

WHAT IS COLLECTIVE INTELLIGENCE?

As a concept, collective intelligence is just what it sounds like. It is the effort to draw on the varied intelligences of many people, using the technologies available to them.

On the one hand, it is nothing new. Collective intelligence, or something like it, was theorized by the likes of Plato, Aristotle, and Thomas Hobbes. And people have been putting their heads together for as long as there have been people; the United States Constitution is a product of collective intelligence, as are so many human achievements, like space flight, which involve the collaboration of many individuals to achieve an established goal.

What makes collective intelligence so compelling now are the technologies that have altered the nature of it—that have made it possible for minds to converge on a problem more easily and efficiently than ever.

Digital technology has not only begun making participation in collective intelligence second-nature to us; our individual intelligences have, in many ways, become secondary to collective intelligence. It is not something we even think twice about.

When we need to summon a fact or a detail, or cannot quite recall a quotation that is just at the back of our minds, we no longer strain to recall it as best we can, or curse our failing memories; we merely reach into our pockets, withdraw our phones, and look up whatever it is we hope to access in that moment. For so many of us in the modern world, to draw on collective intelligence is a banal activity.

This trend will only continue. And we will need it to continue. For the problems that we face today—as a society, and as a species—cannot be surmounted by relying on the old models of work and thought.

THE IMPACT OF COLLECTIVE INTELLIGENCE

The greatest challenge we face today—despite its stark absence from American public discourse—is climate change. The conditions under which the human race came to be and to spread over the globe, over thousands of years, are being upended in the course of a generation. It is hard for us as individuals to wrap our minds around the scale of this, and this difficulty is reflected in our failure to do as much about it as climate scientists have, for years, implored us to do. The Paris Climate Accord is in place, but it is regarded by many as insufficient. We would do more, but roadblocks have been put up by fossil fuel companies and legislators, and people are stubbornly unable or unwilling to accept the urgency of the problem.

And so, the thinking goes, what we need are altogether new solutions to the problem, which sidestep the old roadblocks and present new avenues for problem-solving.

One new solution—or one new mechanism for finding solutions—was presented, earlier this decade, by the MIT Center for Collective Intelligence, when they created the Climate CoLab, which can be accessed online by anyone who wishes to contribute to it. "Any member of the community," explain the creators, "can create a proposal or discuss, support, and evaluate proposals submitted by others. Proposals can advocate new technologies, community projects, marketing strategies, businesses, policies, or any other kind of action to address climate change." Proposals for how to handle climate change are evaluated by other members of the community; just as Wikipedia contributions are edited by volunteers, the Climate CoLab is managed by the same volunteers who come to it in order to contribute.

One of the essential functions of the CoLab is to take the gigantic, sweeping problem of climate change and make it more readily conceivable. Through it, the enormous problem that is climate change gets broken down into "sub-problems" and "defined by three key dimensions: What actions will be taken to address climate change? Where will these actions be taken? And who will take the actions?" The work done there is not confined to the abstract and theoretical; ideas presented there that have gained traction and made an impact in the world include "preparing Vietnamese cities for seasonal migrants, and replacing carbon-intensive diesel pumps used by small farmers in India with foot-operated treadle pumps."[37]

The CoLab is an effort to harness collective intelligence and apply it to the greatest problem we currently face, without letting the effectiveness of that intelligence be inhibited by some of the obstacles to it, which the MIT Center for Collective Intelligence has identified explicitly in their *Handbook of Collective Intelligence*. These include in-group bias, or the tendency for those who

---

37 Laura Fisher, Robert Laubacher, and Thomas W. Malone. "How Millions of People Can Help Solve Climate Change." *PBS Storyline*. January 15, 2014.
http://www.pbs.org/wgbh/nova/next/earth/crowdsourcing-climate-change-solutions/
(accessed March 28, 2018).

participate in a collaborative effort to exclude the thinking of those who stand outside it—which is something that the CoLab and Wikipedia alike would appear to sidestep by simply allowing anyone who wants to contribute.

Other problems include the tendency toward groupthink and the bandwagon effect; collective thinking is not without its potential drawbacks. Indeed, it is inevitable that with advances in technologies that facilitate collective intelligence, ethical considerations arise.[38]

ARTIFICIAL INTELLIGENCE MEETS COLLECTIVE INTELLIGENCE

That is, as we have seen, always the case; virtually any new technology presents, to some extent, an ethical quandary.

The unfortunate tendency of those who use technology is, in so many cases, to put it to misuse prior to putting it to use—to make new technologies destructive before they are used constructively. If we look at our history, we see it again and again: airplanes being used to bomb civilian populations, prior to being used to transport them from place to place; nuclear technology being deployed in bombs well before it is harnessed to generate power. It is anything but inevitable, but it is not exactly unlikely, that world-changing technologies that facilitate collective intelligence—such as *artificial* intelligence—will be used in demonstrably negative ways well before it is used positively.

The imagination runs wild, when we consider how this could manifest itself, in the case of a misapplied artificial intelligence generally. We have decades of science fiction novels, movies, and television shows to help stoke it, with their visions of ruthlessly efficient police robots who act according to the racial and socioeconomic biases of their creators; and a worldwide network of military machines, all of them operated through a computerized central nervous system that can turn on a dime and virtually wipe us out.

---

38 MIT Center for Collective Intelligence. "Handbook of Collective Intelligence." *http://scripts.mit.edu/~cci/HCI/index.php* (accessed March 28, 2018).

The *Terminator* films have reached vast audiences of people, and so many people have seen harrowing visions of AI gone horribly wrong.

There is no way, at this point, to measure the destructive capacity of artificial intelligence, nor to predict exactly how it might be used to our detriment. But we can look to its applications in collective intelligence as a way to begin to envision it.

COLLECTIVE INTELLIGENCE
MEETS ARTIFICIAL INTELLIGENCE

Just as artificial intelligence will come to inflect every aspect of our lives, in ways that are visible to us and invisible, it will influence how our collective intelligence operates, as a kind of unseen hand that enables us to work together more efficiently.

Imagine a conference call in which every utterance is overheard by a virtual assistant and checked for accuracy. Your colleague boasts about something they have accomplished recently, only to have a Siri or Alexa chime in and correct them.

Imagine being on that same conference call, and trying to make a point you have in mind, when you abruptly lose your train of thought. You laugh off this momentary lapse, only to have your digital assistant whisper in your ear where it was you were going with the point you were trying to make.

The involvement of AI in a real-time conversation could be wonderfully helpful; we might live to see a perfectly evenhanded AI moderator who will prevent anyone from dominating a conversation, speaking too long at the expense of other participants, or taking credit for someone else's idea or insight.

It could be a wonderful benefit to those of us in the working world, a great equalizing innovation. This technology could, however, prove to misguide us as much as it could help us; what if the AI that gets innovated merely reflects the unfortunate biases of its creator?

Or, it could turn out that to not have a computerized intelligence sitting in on our conversations and collaborations, and looking over our shoulders, has a certain value that is lost as soon as we introduce it there. We might quickly come to miss not having an AI assistant present at all times, as it somehow gets in the way of our truly reaching one another.

As hard as it can be to envision just how our ethics will be compromised by these technologies, it is essential that we try to do exactly that, despite our tendency as a society / species to do exactly the opposite. As John Gray put it,

> The core of the belief in progress is that human values and goals converge in parallel with our increasing knowledge. The twentieth century shows the contrary. Human beings use the power of scientific knowledge to assert and defend the values and goals they already have. New technologies can be used to alleviate suffering and enhance freedom. They can, and will, also be used to wage war and strengthen tyranny. Science made possible the technologies that powered the industrial revolution. In the twentieth century, these technologies were used to implement state terror and genocide on an unprecedented scale. Ethics and politics do not advance in line with the growth of knowledge—not even in the long run.[39]

Throughout history, we see the same lessons learned and swiftly forgotten, the same self-sabotaging tendencies manifested over and over.

Even as I write this, a scandal is in the process of erupting, in which Facebook has been found to have collaborated with the firm Cambridge Analytica, to the possible detriment of our democratic process. Personal data fell into the hands of those who were not permitted to have it. The implications have not yet been fully discerned.

By the time this book reaches its audience, it may turn out not to be so catastrophic as all that—but it tells us, once again, that the onward march of technology has outpaced our efforts to negotiate its effects on us. We

---

39 John Gray. "Joseph Conrad, Our Contemporary." *Heresies: Against Progress and Other Illusions*. London: Granta UK. 2004.

must confront the potential for large-scale abuses of technology before those abuses take place, or else there might be no way to prevent them.

One source of hope is that just as collective intelligence provides us with the means to confront the problem of climate change, it might similarly help us to undertake a thorough consideration of the ethical implications of social media and data collection.

It could be that the data mining complex that currently monitors and records all that we do online is as unique and perplexing a problem as climate change; that it requires collective thinking just in order to start to find a way through it. Perhaps what we need is a CoLab for every problem we are aware of but have a hard time articulating a clear and straightforward solution to: a CoLab for how we can limit data mining; and a CoLab for safeguarding our democratic process.

COLLABORATIVE RESEARCH

A friend of mine, Steve Barbeaux, is a marine biologist with the National Oceanic and Atmospheric Administration. His work demonstrates some of the benefits of harnessing collective intelligence, and what our work will start to look like in the near future.

For one thing, Steve is physically in the Pacific Northwest, but he could do much of his work anywhere, and the people he works with on a daily basis might be in the same building, but might be as far away as Korea. As he works, Steve relies on people who are vastly disparate in terms of their professional affiliations, levels of work experience, geographical locations, and backgrounds. If he is working on a study of the life history of Pacific cod, for example, he might enlist someone in-house to do maturity studies, hire a private contractor to do research, involve a postdoctoral fellow doing relevant research at a university, and others still, to contribute in the specific ways they are equipped to do. Any specific study he is conducting, for the purposes of the government, or in the ongoing pursuit of his research, might overlap with the work being done by any number of scientists and scholars.

And so he can consult with them, rely on their expertise, or hire them to pitch in whatever way they can, before they move onto other pursuits.

It is something like a catch-and-release model for performing work, and while, as Steve has assured me, this is commonplace in academia and the sciences, it is relatively new to the private sector. There, the tendency is for a company, when hiring someone new, to put that person through a rigorous interview process before offering them benefits and a salary, hoping they stay on indefinitely. Like a fisherman who relies on his trade for sustenance, he hangs on to whatever he can catch for as long as he can.

Soon, we will all be working more like my friend Steve and his colleagues; we will not be caught by the big business fishermen and tossed in a bucket, to live out our days in the smallest of pools. Rather, we will be free to swim at large, offer what we can, momentarily, to those who need us, and be set free again, to offer our expertise elsewhere. The fundamentals of this sort of work are bound to be adopted in the private sector and beyond, as the same principles that have informed the work of scientists come to inform the work of everyone.

Let us not forget that the Internet, which facilitates our efforts at collaboration so well, was created as a tool for governments and universities. Perhaps the transformation of all intellectual work to better fit the governmental/academic model is a case of chickens coming home to roost.

MAKING COLLECTIVE INTELLIGENCE A GAME

You may, at one time, have played a computer game called Foldit, developed at the University of Washington, by the Center for Game Science and the Department of Biochemistry. Released in 2008, it is a puzzle game. The player is faced with a bizarre-looking, three-dimensional ribbon-like structure, with many spokes coming off of it at all angles. The player can manipulate the spokes, and reorient them in whatever way they like, with the goal of producing new connections between them and novel orientations of ribbon and spokes.

The ribbon and spokes have meaning, in ways in which the components of puzzle games often do not. They represent protein structures. By playing the game, and solving the puzzles, the player explores diverse ways in which cellular protein structures come together and form larger structures.

The Center for Game Science offers a concise enough explanation of that protein structures are: "Proteins are small 'machines' within our bodies that handle practically all functions of living organisms. By knowing more about the 3D structure of proteins (or how they 'fold'), we can better understand their function, and we can also get a better idea of how to combat diseases, create vaccines, and even find novel biofuels."

The game was a means for drawing the time and attention of its many disparate users, in order to help scientists better predict the formation of protein structures. "The game evaluates how good of a fold the player has made, and gives them a score. Scores are uploaded to a leaderboard, allowing for competition between players from all around the world." The puzzles increase in difficulty, and all the while the player is helping to solve a long-standing biochemical problem, having to do with predicting the formation of protein structures.

The example of Foldit indicates some of the possibilities of collective intelligence, and what we can accomplish when we properly harness it. In just ten days, the 57,000 players that Foldit first attracted solved a biochemistry problem that scientists had wrestled with for more than a decade. The results, according to the Center for Game Science, "were reported in *Nature* journal, marking the first time the leading scientific journal has published a paper with over 57,000 authors, [the] vast majority of whom have no background in biochemistry."[40]

It is an ingenious way to harness collective intelligence—to make it fun, by making it a game. It sounds like something out of *Mary Poppins*, but for the digital era; it takes a complex problem, and reduces it to its essentials, making it accessible and solvable to those who do not even have particular

---

40 Center for Game Science. "Foldit."
   http://centerforgamescience.org/blog/portfolio/foldit/ (accessed April 12, 2018).

expertise in the field in which the problem emerged. Foldit draws on the problem-solving skills of a vast number of people, crowdsourcing their time and energy and putting it in the service of a noble purpose. It is a strong indication of what masses of people are capable of when they are presented with purposeful work, even when it is entirely voluntary.

SWARM INTELLIGENCE

One outgrowth of collective intelligence is swarm intelligence—something that has been discussed among technologists for quite a long time, but which has taken on a new significance with recent advancements in digital technology and artificial intelligence.

The concept is based on observable behaviors in certain organisms, like ants; as an individual, an ant isn't good for very much. It can lift heavy things, relative to its size, and it can move about on its little legs. Aside from that, it is a fairly helpless creature. As a member of a colony, however, an ant is tremendously capable; the ant and its colony-mates can dig complex structures underground, locate distant food sources and communicate to one another the best way to reach them, build bridges, and so many other things.

Swarm intelligence applies similar logic to human activity, taking individuals who, even when they are very capable, are generally only very good at a handful of things, and pooling their abilities with those of others.

A company called Unanimous AI has developed algorithms that help people make accurate predictions, and have found remarkable success with outcomes like winners of athletic contests. They take the input offered up by many individuals, one after another, and aggregate their input progressively, so that every individual's thinking is made part of a great wave of thought, one data point informing the next, considered concurrently in a lightning-fast fashion. This technology allows not only for the pooling of resources, but for the honing of those resources—a prediction made by one person is altered and perfected by the one who follows, and so on.

That may be hard to visualize. A handy, tangible visual aid is provided by drone swarms, and the technology that governs their movements. Drone swarms are just what they sound like—assemblies of many drones that move through space in a coordinated fashion. Swarm intelligence helps the drones to communicate with one another and make split-second decisions about how to go about working together to accomplish what they are tasked with.

They can be tasked with doing virtually any number of things. The Chinese company Ehang produced a swarm of drones that put on a swarm intelligence-driven light show, capable of improvising and correcting errors as they flew.[41]

Drone swarm technology has also been seized upon by the military and weaponized. In early 2017, the Department of Defense issued a press release describing its Perdix microdrones, which were deployed in a swarm numbering 103. William Roper, of the Strategic Capabilities Office, was quoted as saying,

> Due to the complex nature of combat, Perdix are not pre-programmed synchronized individuals, they are a collective organism, sharing one distributed brain for decision-making and adapting to each other like swarms in nature...Because every Perdix communicates and collaborates with every other Perdix, the swarm has no leader and can gracefully adapt to drones entering or exiting the team.

Perdix drones are meant to be launched from a fighter jet and deployed to carry out tasks that older technologies cannot accomplish.[42] A fleet of miniature drones could go places soldiers and larger vehicles could not, and without endangering the lives of personnel, at least not on the side of those

41 Scott Simonson. "How Swarm Intelligence Is Making Simple Tech Much Smarter." *SingularityHub*. February 8, 2018. *https://singularityhub.com/2018/02/08/how-swarm-intelligence-is-making-simple-tech-much-smarter/* (accessed April 12, 2018).

42 US Department of Defense. "Department of Defense Announces Successful Micro-Drone Demonstration." January 9, 2017. *https://www.defense.gov/News/News-Releases/News-Release-View/Article/1044811/department-of-defense-announces-successful-micro-drone-demonstration/* (accessed April 12, 2018).

who control the drones.

It is tempting to shrug and say that swarm intelligence was bound to be taken up by the military; they already use large, remotely piloted drones to carry out surveillance and bombing raids; and there is no reason to expect them not to put swarm intelligence to use. And it isn't as if nations other than the United States are about to hold back from developing the same technology.

At the Guangzhou Airshow, in China, in 2017, drones flown by a private company, using swarm intelligence, demonstrated what such drones could be capable of, if each one were outfitted with a payload of explosives.[43] At a Russian airbase in Syria, it was reported that more than a dozen drones appeared, carrying explosives and descending on the personnel there. They neutralized the drones, using conventional weapons and jamming technology, but

> The National Academy notes that most of the counterstrategies that the Army has developed are "based on jamming radio frequency and GPS signals." The thinking was: Drones needed those information flows to navigate effectively. Cut them off and you neutralize the attack. But, as more decision-making intelligence gets baked into groups of these systems, those techniques will become less effective.[44]

Simply put, drones may be dangerous in themselves, but when infused with swarm intelligence their lethality increases exponentially, as it makes them harder to stop.

And so, drones that use swarm intelligence are already being put to destructive purposes, like piloted drones before them. There is no indication I know of that there will be a public outcry against explosive-laden drone

43 Elsa Kania. "Swarms at War: Chinese Advances in Swarm Intelligence." *The Jamestown Foundation.* July 6, 2017. *https://jamestown.org/program/ swarms-war-chinese-advances-swarm-intelligence/* (accessed April 12, 2018).

44 Alexis C Madrigal. "Drone Swarms Are Going to Be Terrifying and Hard to Stop." *The Atlantic.* March 7, 2018. *https://www.theatlantic.com/technology/archive/ 2018/03/drone-swarms-are-going-to-be-terrifying/555005/* (accessed April 12, 2018).

swarms before they are deployed more aggressively. I mention it mostly to observe that this is another new technology that has been put to destructive use well before it has been put to work constructively; that swarms of drones have already been developed for use on the battlefield well before we have seen them do anything else.

We are likely to see swarms of drones firing machineguns together in a coordinated, efficient fashion before we see them scatter into a wilderness area, to find a hiker who has gone missing in a national park, or put out a forest fire. But it does not have to be this way. Given the political will and organization, we can reverse this tendency, and see technology like this make our world a little brighter before it makes it a little dimmer.

THE DELIBERATORIUM, WAZE, AND EQUITY THROUGH COLLECTIVE INTELLIGENCE

Thomas Malone is the head of MIT's Center for Collective Intelligence, and he has spoken with great enthusiasm of the potential for collective intelligence to change the way we think and operate.

He has also, though, discussed the potential for collective stupidity—for technologies to make our thinking and working collective in ways that only degrades the way we work and limits whatever potential we, as individuals, bring to a given group.[45]

Whenever I think of what that would mean, I cannot help thinking of the difficulty women often face in predominantly male workplaces, where their contributions are so often marginalized, if not drowned out altogether. Valuable contributions from women can be ignored or overlooked, and while that is often thanks to an active effort to discourage their participation and accomplishment, it is not always necessarily something anyone intends to happen. We all bring to the conference room biases and predispositions that

---

are imprinted upon us, and many people have not done the hard work of examining themselves and rooting out the sexism they inherit from their parents or absorb from the culture at large. When I hear the phrase "collective stupidity," I think of all the great insights and ideas that have gone by the wayside simply because the ones who gave voice to them were not listened to, for the worst possible reasons.

I think, too, of an ingenious strategy for overcoming similar problems that I read about in an article by Juliet Eilperin in *The Washington Post*. The problem, in this case, was that women in the Obama administration were, when meeting with the president, giving voice to valuable ideas only to have the credit for those ideas taken away by their male colleagues. And so, "they devised a strategy called "amplification" to hammer across one another's points during meetings. After one woman offered an idea, if it wasn't acknowledged, another woman would repeat it and give her colleague credit for suggesting it." That way, it could not be left on the table for a male colleague—or anyone who didn't generate it—to take credit for it.[46] It was a simple, commonsense way in which to correct one of the more troubling side effects of getting people together to talk out a problem—the capacity for someone's contribution to be lost or misattributed.

I want to be careful. I don't want to suggest that the Center for Collective Intelligence is doing just the same thing, or something better, as what these female officials did. That would risk doing one of the things they were trying to safeguard against—having their contributions attributed wrongly to others, or having their innovation subsumed by a different one. But it is worth pointing out that the Center's efforts are moving in the same direction: taking the imperfections that arise whenever people come together and talk, and ensuring that the results of those collaborations are not marred by some of the inevitable complications.

---

46 Juliet Eilperin. "How a White House women's office strategy went viral." *The Washington Post*. October 25, 2016. *https://www.washingtonpost.com/news/ powerpost/wp/2016/10/25/how-a-white-house-womens-office-strategy-went-viral/* (accessed April 15, 2018).

What the White House officials did was correct for a certain kind of collective stupidity, and this is part of what the Center does. They identify extant examples of collective intelligence at work—like Google, which, as it pools the vast resources of the World Wide Web, helps make us far more capable as individuals as we would otherwise be—and create new ways to harness collective intelligence. These include the CoLab, which has been used to address many aspects of the vast and complex problem of climate change. They also include the Deliberatorium.

The Deliberatorium is intended to help us work around certain unhelpful tendencies that arise when we come together to solve a problem. We tend, for example, to group ourselves together with those who are most likely to see eye-to-eye with us—think of your Twitter feed, if you have one, which, if you do, is likely to be a collection of people whose views are more or less in accordance with yours. The Deliberatorium also takes into consideration the inability or unwillingness of many people, when considering arguments against or in favor of something, to filter out noise, and privilege arguments that make sense over those that plainly don't.

The scientists behind the Deliberatorium have posited that the reason for these and other problems with the ways in which we generally deliberate and argue is that the conversations we have are bound to time, rather than to any other organizing principle. The last person to speak in a conversation is often the one whose voice resonates the most, simply because they were the last one to say anything. A conversation can undulate as it proceeds, and things can get lost; this can have adverse effects on the results of that conversation.

One of the tools the Deliberatorium uses is argument mapping. It takes an entire conversation and organizes it, so that the ideas that arose in it can be more fairly evaluated. It removes a conference from the strictures of time and gives them another organizing principle altogether. It eliminates repetition of ideas, which can artificially inflate their significance. It organizes problems so that they link directly to proposed solutions, which link directly to details of those solutions and problems that might arise as they are implemented. It takes all the messiness of collaboration and attempts to clean it up.[47]

The Deliberatorium is, by today's standards, old; its innovation dates to ten years ago. If the work that it performed were to be updated, done by artificial intelligence and deployed universally, then perhaps when we hung up, at the end of a conference call, we might be sent, moments later, a message with a summary of the call attached, so that all of its contents are reorganized and made clearer and plainer. All of the noise and repetition would be filtered out of this call summary. The unhelpful tangents and grandstanding by the participant who had no ideas of his own, but still had the most to say, would not appear anywhere in the summary, making way for the briefer, more helpful comments by the call's more reserved but more savvy participant. The best ideas that arose could be plainer; the bad ideas that sounded good at the time could be exposed for the bad ideas they are.

It isn't hard to imagine how such a technology could go wrong. If the one who develops the automated argument mapper is one of the same guys who talks at length but has nothing to contribute to conversations, generally, then the system could wrongly privilege statements that are, in fact, unhelpful. It could be a sophisticated tool that only serves to reflect the biases of its creator, increasing collective stupidity, which is exactly the thing it is meant to safeguard against. This is the sort of thing that only helps to emphasize the need for transparency in such innovations, and reminds us of the need to make such ethical considerations.

But we can witness the effects of such sharing of information in our morning and evening commutes. The Waze app is an ingenious innovation that allows us to pool our observations as we drive to warn others about what lies on the road ahead. It allows us to report potholes, cars stranded on the side of the road, construction zones, and the presence of the highway patrol. It makes it possible for us to protect one another from driving hazards, and do it with great ease. It is collective intelligence applied to the

---

47 "Introduction to the MIT Deliberatorium." YouTube video, 9:27, posted by Mark Klein. September 7, 2008. https://www.youtube.com/watch?time_continue=370&v=31Ipljh_Zsg

roads we drive on and how we traverse them—and if it can make our driving that much safer and easier, imagine what, when it is applied to other aspects of our lives, it can help us accomplish.

BUSINESS CONSTELLATIONS

Collective intelligence will soon affect our everyday lives, and inform how we operate at the workplace; as we have observed, it is already beginning to do so. There has been an analogous realignment at a larger scale, too, in the ways in which businesses relate to one another—how they compete and work together.

Just as a constellation is a group of stars that are grouped together to form meaningful patterns in the night sky, we could call a business constellation a group of businesses that temporarily align around a significant purpose. More and more, companies are coming together to complement each other and cooperate towards a broad objective.

This differs rather dramatically from traditional business partnerships, in terms of its impact and number of collaborators. Companies are partnering in leveraging services, aggregating solutions, changing regulations, and helping one another to achieve bigger results. Business constellations are conceptual networks of individuals and businesses that get together to solve a problem or innovate with no or low formality. Businesses come together and break apart at the same speed, and make considerable progress in critical areas of social, moral, economic, and technological development. Companies can be part of multiple constellations at same time, and collaborate on different projects in order to serve multiple purposes.

Living as we are in the Fourth Industrial Revolution, we need to reassess our knowledge of how businesses interact, compete, and collaborate. Digital and new technologies are disrupting companies, business channels, business models, jobs, and entire industries. At the same time, new generations of people are coming to the workplace, bringing with them unheard-of mentalities and understandings of relationship models. These young people are willing to collaborate, rather than to compete, and they want to make a difference. The convergence of these forces will demolish received business structures, revise old patterns of supply-demand dominance, and create entirely new ecosystems.

Accordingly, new business models have surged in recent years, and new terms have been coined to define them. "Frenemies" are companies that compete in one area and are business partners in another. Samsung, for example, manufactures most iPhone screens, and yet is the largest manufacturer of Android phones, making Apple its archrival on smartphones and its most prominent customer at the same time. Amazon and Microsoft recently announced Gluon, a partnership to deliver a new software tool for developers that makes it easier for them to build AI/machine learning systems. Both are the most significant contenders on cloud computing solutions, but they need help to fight Google in that space.

"Customer-Partner" is another model that boomed along with tech growth in development of the cloud. On these networks, a company can be simultaneously a user of one product, a reseller of your solutions, and a partner on developing your technology. One example of this is Azure, Microsoft's cloud computing platform. A partner can use Azure to develop software solutions and sell them to its customer base. Those solutions might live in their own websites or transact in Microsoft's marketplace. That same partner, however, might also resell Office 365, and use it as their productivity solution. In that case, the partner will be at the same time a customer of Microsoft SaaS and IaaS, and a partner on PaaS. This increases mutual dependency between companies, and results in a complex, interconnected business environment that would have been unheard of in prior eras.

"Business ecosystems" are created around big companies that offer market-wide strategic solutions. Amazon is one unavoidable example of a big business ecosystem anchor. It is a large, constantly growing, and highly successful company that relies for its success on a vast array of actors who contribute to that success in unique ways. As Haydn Shaughnessy wrote in Forbes, the "Amazon ecosystem," as it applies to books, is "made up of merchants, writers, reviewers, publishers, apps developers, and the information market of commentators, analysts, journalists and feature writers who get the word out about opportunity on the Amazon platform." Every one of these entities works toward the success of the Amazon ecosystem, and they depend on it at the same time. "All these people need to develop their own capabilities in order to succeed on the Amazon platform. To participate you need to be capable of growing and adapting, and of course competing—all the while putting your trust in Amazon's ability to make the right moves."[48]

One potential drawback to this is that it leaves a great deal of power in the hands of Amazon; if its interest turn toward developing and maintaining a monopoly, at the expense of the interests of some of its contributors, then there is not much anyone can do to stop them. But the sheer number of contributors to Amazon's success safeguards it against failure, in the case of one or some of those contributors failing to live up to expectations, at the same time that everyone wants to contribute their best work, in the name of Amazon thriving, and improving the whole ecosystem.

The arrangement is altogether new. It indicates the appeal, to those who belong to younger generations, of collaborative work that is driven by a sense of purpose. People want to express their points of view, voice their passions, and be part of something bigger than themselves. Business ecosystems offer a way to harness their energy—to honor their needs and desires, and make the most of the sheer scale of their thinking. It is that kind of energy that has brought about the business constellation, and the continued reorientation of how we understand the way businesses work together.

---

48 Shaughnessy, Haydn. "Why Amazon Succeeds." *Forbes*. April 29, 2012. *https://www.forbes.com/sites/haydnshaughnessy/2012/04/29/why-amazon-succeeds/* (accessed April 11, 2018).

COLLECTIVE INTELLIGENCE AND COLLECTIVE PURPOSE

Soon, we will work together in ways that many of us currently do not—laboring in concert all the way, and relying on collective intelligence as readily as we do our individual faculties.

At the same time, as we have seen, we will come to our work out of a compelling sense of purpose, and not only out of sheer necessity. We will work in the company of likeminded others, as we labor not only to gain as much material wealth as we can, but in the name of some compelling purpose that brings us to our physical or virtual collaborative working space.

These are two ways in which new technologies will serve to humanize us. They will make our lives better by making us more likely to work for what matters, rather than only for what we need. And they will ensure that we do it in the name of social equity. They will ensure that this equity is something we can sustain. We can look forward to a future in which our working lives, generally, make more sense.

CROWDSOURCING

Perhaps the most readily available example of collective intelligence, which we've failed to mention so far, is crowdsourcing. It's become so familiar, it's easy to take it for granted—how we can be stumped on a difficult question, then pull out our phone, open Twitter or Facebook, and ask virtually everyone we know for help solving it.

It takes minutes. People crowdsource reading recommendations, solutions to computer-related technical problems, puzzles embedded in video games, and countless other things.

Crowdsourcing is, as per Merriam-Webster, "the practice of obtaining needed services, ideas, or content by soliciting contributions from a large group of people and especially from the online community rather than from traditional employees or suppliers." Crowdsourcing is a means of sharing information, a way to democratize knowledge and make the hard-won intellectual resources of the best-educated people available to anyone and everyone.

In a similar way, crowdfunding is one way in which people draw on the financial resources of others in order to meet their specific needs. If someone needs money, they can start a GoFundMe drive, and accrue the funds they need for a heart transplant, or whatever expensive but necessary thing they have to have but can't afford.

This approach does draw criticism, especially in light of other industrialized nations that offer universal healthcare, and don't leave it up to their citizens to hope they know enough people who have enough money between them to buy them new hearts. Yet it is worth standing back for a moment and admiring how an online tool has been used to save lives that would have otherwise been lost. It brings out the best in people, asking them to act on their morals, their empathy, and their compassion.

There is potential in this. We have proven that people are willing to come together to give strangers the means to go on living.

The twin phenomena of crowdfunding and crowdsourcing provide us all the evidence we need, that collective intelligence is on the rise. And as it rises, it will give people new incentives to improve themselves. It isn't something that will be done for its own sake, but for the sake of many. People will want to improve their stations in life so that they have the most to contribute elsewhere.

The more skilled an individual is, the more that person has to offer. That, of course, has long been the case, but skills have been quantified in ways that are approximations at best.

Perhaps you have a master's degree in software engineering. Whether you earned that degree in 2018 or 1998 makes an enormous difference in what you potentially have to offer the world of software engineering today. If you have kept up with the monumental changes to the software landscape since 1998, then congratulations, you are a great resource. If you haven't, though—or you haven't been very diligent about it, and have only learned exactly what you've needed to, to keep your job—you effectively have nothing to offer the world at large.

While this is an extreme example, it illustrates not only the need to stay up to date in one's field, but the new incentive to do so. When crowdsourcing is not only commonplace, but comes to characterize the way we do our work, then the people who continue to educate themselves, and do the work necessary to staying relevant, will be the ones who have the most to contribute.

The better and more diverse your skills, the more opportunities you will have, like those people who work at every Olympic games, who have the opportunity to do so because they can speak multiple languages, often in more than one idiom. Their education makes this work possible. Even on the lower end of jobs—theirs is temporary work, after all—this is the case.

We are witnessing, in this way, the emergence of an altogether novel reason to seek education beyond attaining a degree. It is a new imperative for fostering a healthy reputation: to increase an individual's ability to contribute to the causes that matter to them most. And when people seek education, everyone wins, as education is the most potent builder of social equity, the most reliable means by which people can uplift themselves and thereby uplift everyone.

Thanks to things like crowdfunding, crowdsourcing, and collective intelligence, that reality is plainer than ever; it is utterly demystified. The connection between the resources of one and the benefits of many are laid bare, and the path to sustainable social equity is plainer than ever.

CHAPTER FIVE:

Sustainability through Social Equity

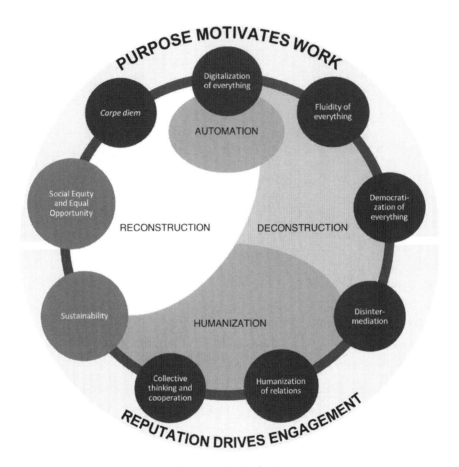

Figure 8. Trends
Source: CollectiveBrains

THIS BRINGS US TO ANOTHER POINT on our Trends chart, and one of the most essential aspects of the coming changes to our economy, something that should be one of our primary concerns in the years to come.

For an astonishingly long time, sustainability has not been a primary concern, as we can see in deforestation, and in the rise of fossil fuels and the climate change it has brought on. And so, we must pay attention to the sustainability of things, most particularly the collaborative, purpose-driven work we do.

People are going to make an awful lot more money. With the emergence of AI, the expansion of collective intelligence, and the boost that automation will give to the productivity of those in the workforce, the imminent creation of a vast amount of new wealth should be treated as a given.

And so there are some essential, pressing questions we ought to consider. Whose wealth will it be, when it is generated? How will it be distributed? And how can we ensure the greatest equity for those in our society, rather than a greater concentration of wealth in the hands of a select few people, and dwindling opportunities for everyone else?

Because one of the great risks, as we make our way through the meat grinder of the Fourth Industrial Revolution, is that we will only see wealth further consolidated at the top stratum of our society; that our billionaires will soon be trillionaires, and the ranks of the unemployed will expand, as automation eliminates job after job after job.

The vast creation of new wealth is inevitable. Its even and equable distribution is anything but. With things the way they are now—the gap between rich and poor expanding all the time, and more and more wealth consolidated among elites—it might seem as if an increase in social equity is not exactly a likely outcome of the changes in our economy.

But an increase in equity is exactly what lies ahead of us. This is what we have to learn from previous industrial revolutions—in which, time and again, after a period of turmoil and disruption, a new equilibrium comes about, one that is decidedly better for everyday people.

Things can get very bad—and I do not want to risk eliding the damage that can be done, the jobs that can be lost, the houses that can be foreclosed on, and the hopelessness that can set in. Because we in the United States have such a threadbare social safety net, the rise of artificial intelligence is likely to ruin people's lives.

History is a great teacher. If we study it, we see, time and again, that with every surge in technology, and every industrial revolution, great turmoil results from the social and economic upheavals. But in the wake of that disruption is a better quality of life for everyone. In the long run, lives improve.

And so there is hope. On the other side of the suffering ahead—the layoffs, the bankruptcies—is something better than what we have now. It can be tempting to be skeptical, even cynical, but we have every reason to think that greater social equity is on the horizon.

THE RESTAURANT OF THE FUTURE

The new wealth will not come out of thin air. It will be squeezed out of industries and business sectors that are right in front of our faces. AI and Big Data will combine to transform and empower every person, organization, and process in the world—across all economic fields—making them more efficient, more productive, and more cost-effective, all at once.

We can think of implementing these technologies as something like switching on a giant machine that in one fell swoop eliminates all the world's little inefficiencies—like air being sucked out of a vacuum-sealed bag.

This will work on the large scale, at multinational corporations, and on the small scale, at small businesses. Take, for example, the humble neighborhood restaurant.

It is no small task, to create a profitable restaurant operation, considering the high operating costs that come with such a business, like utilities and salary costs, to name just two. It is a labor-intensive business, and in order to make it lucrative, a manager/owner must acquire a loyal customer base and keep them happy. They must control costs like utilities and kitchenware, yet buy proper ingredients at the right quantity and quality. They have to manage payroll, with flexible schedules and employee turnover. The chef must stay motivated and innovative, and the place has to be clean and look nice.

I have always wanted to open a restaurant. Think of the constant challenges: the need to be aware of every development at your establishment; to lead your staff and keep them motivated and happy; to greet your customers with a friendly face and keep them coming back. From afar, it seems to be a 24/7 commitment, something that cannot be done without full engagement—which is why I haven't done it. Three decades from now, though, perhaps I could. Maybe I will.

The same neighborhood restaurant will be run using a spectrum of new technologies. Big data companies, in cooperation with one another, will accumulate and integrate new fields of data on our habits and consumption patterns. Whoever wants to open a restaurant, then, can download an app that will help to project demand and target the right audience—something that, if calculated poorly, can doom a new business from the day it opens. The app will cross their customer base habits and aggregated data with the same averages of the ones in their geography. And they will know precisely how many loyal customers come to their store, how frequently they visit, what they consume, the average price paid for wine by the bottle, how many patrons eat dessert, how each menu item is ranked, and how to correct displayed prices in order to make them as attractive as possible. All of these are things that a restauranteur must take into account now, but these decisions are often made based on personal preference, or through a costly process of trial and error. Soon enough, there will be readymade and comprehensive data on every facet of this.

The restaurant owner will know how their customers' behavior changed last year, last month, yesterday, and an hour ago. They will know how their customers rate other restaurants in the region—what they like about them, and what the current establishments are failing to get right. All of this will be automated; it will be a matter of gathering data and applying it, which grows more commonplace all the time.

The same app could even help on the management side of things: breaking down the menu and projecting consumption according to future demand; procuring ingredients at the right quantities, and at the best prices; and getting them delivered in a timely manner. It could do all of this while scheduling employees to be ready to receive those deliveries. The app will help with hiring the appropriate staff for each hour of the day, and with planning waiters' profiles to match the customers' profiles in each period.

It could also balance the hourly rate cost of the staff members with their professional online reviews, and automatically hire the best of the crop the restaurant can afford. The restaurant will have guidelines for innovation, efficient inventory management, and reduced waste and utility consumption. Later, the manager can get information as to where the ideal location is, to open a second store, and a third, and so on.

That little restaurant will be just one automated, AI-powered operation among many, with deliveries being made by driverless trucks or drones, carrying vegetables that are grown through automated agricultural operations, and so on, and on, and on.

Total expenses will be a fraction of what they are at a small restaurant now. The operation will be more efficient than it could possibly be today. Profits for such a business will climb to new heights.

These are some of the inefficiencies that will be ironed out of a small business that employs maybe a dozen people. They are easy to see, but it is harder to visualize, all at once, the effect that similar forces will have on a business that employs 100 people, or 1,000, or 10,000. The same effects will be felt on that larger scale, multiplied many times over.

The world in which these technologies operate will be more efficient. It will function better and make more money for those who stand to profit. It will be wonderful—as long as there are still enough people living in that world who aren't destitute, and can afford to buy whatever it is the newly efficient, AI-powered corporation's subsidiaries produce.

The restaurant of the future cannot stay in business if no one has enough money to go out for a meal, once in a while. It is a thing hardly worth engineering, if the future that rings it in is one in which no one can afford any luxuries whatsoever—where there is no middle class, and hardly a workforce to speak of.

That is the reality we face, if we do not take seriously the need to distribute wealth equably, and to ensure that our future is sustainable. And while we have every reason to think we will all, in the long run, benefit from the innovations that are transforming our economy, we cannot sit back and expect social equity to materialize before us. We must work for it. We must ensure that things change the way we want them to. And that work starts with articulating the world we want to live in, imagining it from the ground up, and setting the terms for the distribution of this new wealth.

OUR SOCIAL SAFETY NET

One clear thing we can do, in order to make the coming upheaval easier on us all, is to bolster the United States's social safety net.

To suggest this may risk seeming to be hopelessly out of touch, given the political climate and the unwillingness to enact this sort of thing on the part of every branch of our federal government. But at the same time, there are rumblings that suggest that such improvements might not be far off, with popular teachers' strikes getting results as far as securing more state funding for education, and increased, genuine interest in a universal healthcare system.

Who knows if any such thing will come into being? But there is likely to be increased demand for it, if the Oxford study was correct when, in 2013, it found that 47 percent of American jobs are at risk of being eliminated, thanks to advances in computerization such as AI.[49] That means that many Americans who are currently employed will lose their jobs; it means that there will be increased demand for a safety net, because the need for it will increase.

As I write, one of the prospective candidates for the 2020 presidential election is Andrew Yang, a former tech company executive who knows what lies ahead of us. He is quoted in the *New York Times* as saying that, with the advent of self-driving trucks, "'We're going to have a million truck drivers out of work who are 94 percent male, with an average level of education of high school or one year of college.'" It will be enough, he says, "'to create riots in the street. And we're about to do the same thing to retail workers, call center workers, fast-food workers, insurance companies, accounting firms.'"

One of Yang's proposals is nothing other than a universal basic income, or what he calls a "Freedom Dividend," which would be sent to every American citizen aged eighteen to sixty-four. This would help to defray the staggering effects of automation.[50]

I cannot say with confidence that Yang has a strong chance at winning a presidential primary, nor that he will succeed at pushing the prospect of a UBI near enough to reality to make it a feasible solution, given the state of American politics. But it does seem absolutely telling, that a businessman turned political novice—of whom there have been many, in years past—arrives to the scene proposing a measure that is designed to benefit everyday people who are the victims of economic forces beyond their control. It indicates that a tide is turning—that certain realities are growing harder to look away from, and solutions to our problems, like a UBI, which were unthinkable ten or twenty years ago, will soon be on the table.

---

49 Carl Benedikt Frey and Michael A. Osborne. "The Future of Employment: How Susceptible Are Jobs to Computerisation?" University of Oxford. September 17, 2013. *https://www.oxfordmartin.ox.ac.uk/downloads/academic/ The_Future_of_Employment.pdf* (accessed May 9, 2018).

50 Kevin Roose. "His 2020 Campaign Message: The Robots Are Coming." *The New York Times.* February 10, 2018. *https://www.nytimes.com/2018/02/10/technology/his-2020-campaign-message-the-robots-are-coming.html* (accessed May 9, 2018).

It would be in everyone's best interests to establish a better social safety net—both the people who will struggle to stay in the workforce, and the people who employ them. The CEOs and business owners will need to have people making a living, so that they can participate in the economy.

It returns us to the dilemma in which you cannot make your business so efficient that you eliminate the entire social stratum of people who buy the things you produce. A robust social safety net only helps to provide stability and sustainability to a system that works. It ensures that people can get educated, so that they don't get left behind by the rapidly changing economy. In a strange way, the interests of socialists and capitalists are bound to align, when adherents to both ideologies realize their vested interest in maintaining a healthy, educated, and empowered workforce.

SOCIAL EQUITY

We must work to increase social equity, and we must ensure that it is sustainable.

I am quite deliberate about using the word "equity," rather than "equality." The former denotes a far more effective approach to resolving inequality than the latter.

When we work toward equality, we generally ensure that everyone has an equal amount of resources of similar quality—that they have access to the same things as everyone else. When we have equity in mind, we recognize that the needs of various people differentiate widely—that to ensure true equity requires seeing to their needs as individuals. Measures that help to guarantee equity take into account the plain fact that deficiencies are unique to every individual.

We all fall short, in our own specific ways, of achieving our ideal circumstances; and so, in order for us to achieve equity, we need systems in place that see to our individual needs. We need, in short, a thriving education system. Perhaps the most important way we can ensure equity is through education, and by guaranteeing everyone's access to it.

It runs counter to true equity to have the wealthy send their children to private schools, where they are educated with far better resources than children at public schools; it is incumbent upon to close the gap between the quality of those two different sorts of educations.

Indeed, equity in education is not something we have, historically, enjoyed. Colleges were once the domains of wealthy, white men; it took many years to break down the barriers that kept women and people of color off of university campuses. Even now, the cost of higher education continues to rise, exceeding the reach of many young people.

And yet, at the same time, education is transforming, manifesting itself in ways that would have been impossible before the digital revolution. College campuses have not yet been bulldozed over, but many classes are offered online, and there are more and more alternatives to such a traditional approach to education. If I want to learn another language, I can enroll in a class, and meet with peers and an instructor in a room full of desks and chairs—or I can download the Duolingo app, and follow a very different path toward mastery of another tongue.

Look, too, at how many people today learn to cook.

If we are lucky, we grew up in the company of excellent cooks who have family recipes and techniques to impart that have been developed over many years, if not generations. But a lot of people have nothing like that to draw on, and they enter their adult lives without an idea how to cook anything more elaborate than canned soup.

Almost universally, now, in order to make up for that deficiency, we turn to cooking blogs for recipes and YouTube videos for instructions on how to dice an onion and hard-boil an egg. And those are incredibly good resources for an education in how to cook; virtually any task involved in preparing food is demonstrated and explained for us, by any number of people who have recorded their instructions. A live human instructor is good if you can get it, but for anyone who can't get it, there are alternatives.

This is, on a small scale, something like the sea change we will see in how members of the next generation go about their educations beyond the kitchen. The way they prepare for their careers will be much more like the way we learn to cook—by preparing for each task as necessary; by slowly accruing a comprehensive education as they are upskilled for every individual project they take on.

THE EDUCATIONS OF GENERATIONS

Education across generations has changed and will continue to change. The relationship between work and education is one we can call the work-education cycle, and if we look at how it has changed recently, we can project what it will look like soon.

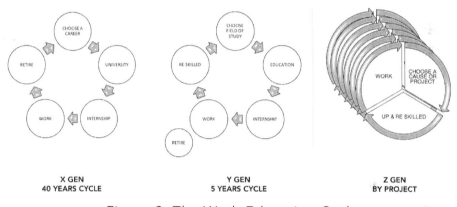

Figure 9. The Work-Education Cycle
Source: CollectiveBrains

The people of Generation X were educated according to a forty-year cycle, one they inherited from prior generations. They chose their professions, undertook educations to prepare for them, and worked in those careers until retirement.

Generation Y focused on a field of study—but, given the pace in technological development, many of them have needed to be reskilled every five years. This is especially the case in the technology industry, where advances are constant and sweeping. For many in this generation, retirement seems more distant all the time.

For Generation Z, education will be undertaken constantly, on demand. A worker will face a specific project that demands altogether new skills; they will have to educate themselves for that project in particular, being reskilled or upskilled again and again, for as many different projects as they want to do.

Soon, everyone's work will change as constantly as that of the software engineer. That is, in fact, a helpful way to think of it; it makes every bit of sense that if you work in technology, which is always advancing, you have to keep educating yourself, in whatever way you can, so that you aren't replaced by someone who is fresh out of school and already up to speed. And this dynamic is abundantly familiar to academics, who attend conferences and subscribe and contribute to specialized periodicals, in order to keep themselves up to speed with the latest research in their fields. As AI brings cutting edge technology to bear on our working lives, every workplace will require some version of this of its employees.

As the need to be constantly educated only grows more urgent, traditional education will continue to recede from our lives. Many members of Generation Y have incurred mortgage-sized debts in order to go to college; it is unlikely that many from Generation Z will want to do the same, and alternative approaches to education are bound to proliferate.

The current way of doing things cannot persist, which seems especially plain when we consider just how quickly what we learn grows outdated. According to a 2016 report by the World Economic Forum, in some tech grad courses, knowledge gained in the first year is outdated by the time students finish their fourth year.[51]

So often, we hear people lament that education is wasted on the young; that it might be better for people to go to college when they're a little older than the typical college student, when their lives are not in such states of confusion, and they can focus. That is exactly what we can expect to see, with

---

51 World Economic Forum. "The Future of Jobs: Employment, Skills and Workforce Strategy for the Fourth Industrial Revolution." January 2016. http://www3.weforum.org/docs/WEF_Future_of_Jobs.pdf (accessed April 27, 2018).

cycles of education and production overlapping throughout every career. We will spend many more hours learning, throughout our lives, than everyone did in the generation that preceded ours.

THE NEW ERA OF EDUCATION

It brings me no joy to reiterate that if you have a white-collar job, you are likely to get laid off from it unexpectedly. If the Oxford study is credible, when it reports that 47 percent of all jobs are at risk of being made obsolete in the near future, then you have something slightly better than a fifty-fifty chance of your job continuing to exist for the next ten or fifteen years.

If and when that layoff happens, you will want to find another job. But if you lost your job to an AI system, many other workers with similar expertise will have also just been laid off. There will only be a few jobs left in your field, which means fierce competition for the few that remain.

If you want to continue to follow anything like the same career path you were on, you will need to develop new productive skills and new competencies. Returning to a university campus, to emerge another two to four years later, newly qualified, simply will not do, as that would be terribly expensive, and you can't afford to take that much time off from your career.

What, then, will you do?

That question is being answered by an array of actors, one of them being the aforementioned Duolingo, the company that has developed an app to teach languages via computer or smartphone, using quizzes, text interaction, and voice recognition software. It promises the same outcome as a university language course—mastery of another language—but without the vast apparatus that comes with a class at a school. Not even a decade into its existence, it offers courses in twenty-eight languages to more than 200 million users worldwide.[52]

Another company, Claned, from Finland, is rethinking education as it is currently done in and out of classrooms. As it is described by the organization

---

52 "Duolingo." *Wikipedia. https://en.wikipedia.org/wiki/Duolingo* (accessed May 9, 2018).

Worlddidac, a trade association for the educational resources industry,

> Claned learning solution gathers data about student interaction with the learning space and aggregates that data to show student performance, learning orientation, and characteristics which can then be used as feedback by teachers. With this data, teachers can tailor their behavior based on student needs for the most effective education for all. In personalized education, the instructor's role has changed to one of designing, orchestrating, and supporting learning experiences (online and those within classrooms and laboratories) rather than requiring all students to listen to the same lectures and complete the same homework in the same sequence and at the same pace. This enables students to learn the required material by building and following their own learning paths.[53]

This innovation transforms rather fundamentally the job of the instructor in a classroom, making it easier for a teacher to track a student's progress and determine what that individual needs in order to succeed in their educations. It eliminates the guesswork from teaching, and supplements a teacher's intuition with hard data, helping to eliminate the influence of prejudice or sheer inefficiency.

Outside of the classroom, this technology allows for a new approach to education, one in which someone learns on an ongoing basis, throughout a career. It can help an employee train for a specific job they are not quite currently prepared for, building on a knowledge base so that they can keep up with their job's constantly shifting expectations.

New education innovations may not be ready to take someone with no knowledge of circuits and make them an electrical engineer. But they could take an experienced project manager and upskill that person so that they are prepared to work in an AI-powered workplace. And in the workplace,

---

53 Worlddidac Association. "Claned—Finnish learning platform challenging the world to learn better." *https://worlddidac.org/news/claned-finnish-learning-platform-challenging-world-learn-better/* (accessed April 27, 2018).

technology like that developed by Claned can keep employees on top of new developments, training them in new areas on the job, keeping them upskilled and reskilled according to an established program.

The challenge is to make the working world as it will come to be into something that is sustainable, where AI does not simply shove human employees off the edge of a cliff and hope they fashion their own parachutes before they hit the ground.

WHAT EQUITY WILL LOOK LIKE

The social equity we are likely to see is not only a matter of resource distribution. In the workplace to come, longstanding wrongs can be put right, or prevented before they even emerge.

Imagine, for example, a workplace that is impervious to discrimination—where unethical, unfair, or discriminatory practices are brought instantaneously to the attention of those who are best equipped to put a stop to them. When workplace interactions are visible to an AI that has been trained to recognize toxic practices, it could be much harder for a manager to get away with them, whether that practice is sexual harassment, or unfairly promoting one employee over another. This is one of the benefits of fracturing the traditional workspace, and allowing people to work from home. It means that interactions between employees are conducted in virtual spaces, via email or some other system. It means that interactions leave digital paper trails, and people can be held accountable for how they treat their colleagues.

Discrimination is bad, first and foremost, because it is unjust. But it is also bad because it is grossly inefficient; it means promoting the wrong people for the wrong reasons.

Discrimination in hiring can be corrected for, as reputations come to be more quantifiable, and candidates are more readily represented by their accomplishments. When a hiring manager looks at someone and sees an online profile, or digitally compiled reputation, that manager will not have the opportunity to let their personal prejudice influence a decision to hire, work with, or sign a contract with that person.

These changes to our working culture will take place only if we strive to bring them into reality; we cannot sit back and expect the future workplace to become more like this as if the weather were shifting. In order to see them come into being, we must take an active interest in the future of work, pushing for legislation and putting pressure on administrators where we work now, to implement new technologies so that they bring their benefits equably. To do this is to make our working lives more sustainable—to make up for those shortcomings that have stood in the way of true equity in the past.

Equity is our goal, and as we strive for it we must look for ways in which we can correct our moral failings as a society, as this is what has stood in the way of such efforts in the past.

At stages in their history, the ancient Greeks strove for such equity, and devoted a great deal of thought to how it could be achieved. But they made the regrettable mistake of dividing themselves into distinct social classes. They even kept slaves. True equity was always out of their reach, despite their best efforts and good intentions.

We must strive for equity, and we must strive for diversity. The 2018 edition of the Global Talent Competitiveness Index (GTCI) report focuses on this explicitly. As the report explains, "In the ethos of standardisation that characterised the 20th century, diversity was problematic, a feature of society largely ignored; today it is increasingly recognised as a resource for innovation and problem solving that we are beginning to tap through collaboration between people with different personalities, knowledge sets, experiences, and perspectives." Throughout, this report is concerned with articulating the many benefits of diversity, and the ways in which many people who are diverse in terms of race, gender, and cognition can collaborate effectively.[54]

At this stage, it can be taken for granted that diversity is good for us; that to have a diverse labor pool, student body, or overall population, is worth

---

54 Bruno Lanvin and Paul Evans, eds. "The Global Talent Competitiveness Index 2018: Diversity for Competitiveness." December 2017. *https://gtcistudy.com/wp-content/uploads/2018/01/GTCI-2018-web.r1-1.pdf* (accessed May 9, 2018).

striving for. One of the great benefits of advances in AI is that it can help remove barriers to diversity, reducing the influence of a hiring manager's prejudice, or the hiring policies of a company that are not intended to downplay diversity but do so inadvertently.

Innovations can help promote diversity in many locales where it currently holds us back. Education is just one of them. Traditional education systems have focused on uniformity and standardization: uniform aims, identical content, standardized learning progression, undifferentiated amount of time assigned for learning, and common criteria for success—regardless of the diversity of talents in the student population. The emphasis has been on the homogeneity of learners, as well as outcomes. This paradigm has long required that learners are seen as similar in many ways, and that differences were deliberately not acknowledged.

This approach may have been necessary, at a time when education was being expanded, when public schools were being established and education was made available to more people than ever. In the modern world, though, it is untenable. It is common for teachers to be faced with classes filled with people from a diverse range of backgrounds, cultures, learning preferences, and abilities.

There is ample evidence from the OECD's Programme for International Student Assessment (PISA) test that diversity matters—but perhaps not always in the way we hope it will. Students with immigrant backgrounds perform less well on average on the PISA assessment than their native peers; those from wealthier families outperform the less wealthy; and there are long-standing gender differences in performance that, on average, favor boys (in mathematics) and girls (in reading). And while these performance gaps are critical, the significant variation in their magnitude across countries indicates that these differences can be largely mitigated, if not overcome. Providing all students with the skills and competencies required to thrive in school and beyond means being able to meet their diverse sets of needs.

Teachers need to be able to adapt learning activities to the different abilities, competencies, and student motivations. They must make the lessons they offer suit the students' linguistic, cultural, and social backgrounds. The effort to do that must be complemented with a sensitive assessment that allows learner strengths and weaknesses to be identified. Technology plays a crucial role in permitting the individualization of information, communication, and materials. Investments must be made to equip and train the education ecosystem.

CREATIVE WORK AND AUTOMATION

We can think of the future of work as a kind of spectrum. At one end of the spectrum will be those who are fully up-to-speed with developments in the workplace, who are consistently reskilled and upskilled so that they can function as modern laborers. They are the ones who will manage AI systems, for one thing, and there will be relatively few of them.

At the other, more highly populated end of the spectrum will be people who do an altogether different sort of labor, whose working lives are devoted to ensuring the prosperity and wellbeing of others.

As robots and AI take over the workplace, people will be freer to be more fully human. Liberated from jobs and tasks that fail to harness their full potential, they will engage in a more humanized sort of work. They will do the things that machines and AI cannot do—or cannot do as well as human beings.

On the one hand, this includes creative work—work that requires an active and fertile imagination. Certain kinds of strategic thinking will always be the province of human beings, as is work that involves raw creativity.[55] This is certainly not limited to, but includes the work of artists and writers.

There have been experiments with computer programs that are designed to write novels, and some have opined that the job of the novelist can be automated. But there will always be a certain value placed in the author, and

---

55 Joseph Pistrui. "The Future of Human Work Is Imagination, Creativity, and Strategy." *Harvard Business Review*. January 18, 2018. *https://hbr.org/2018/01/the-future-of-human-work-is-imagination-creativity-and-strategy* (accessed May 9, 2018).

the humanity of that author.

People may find they enjoy the machine-written novels of the future, which could be written instantaneously and churned out of publishing houses with ruthless efficiency. But we are as likely to want to read those novels as we are to crowd into arenas to watch sports played by mechanical people. The basketball robots could, perhaps, perform at levels human beings never could. They would not tire out, get injured, need to take breaks, or even stop to have a drink of water. But there would be something fundamental missing from that contest, the lack of which would ruin the whole spectacle—a certain fallibility, or fundamental humanness that we want to identify with. As superior to humans, in so many ways, as a machine can be, there are things we will stubbornly insist on keeping human.

At the moment of writing, Google has just announced an upgrade to their email system that allow for the autocompletion of entire messages from person to person. They have similarly demonstrated technology that can convincingly simulate a user's voice as they call to make an appointment for a haircut.

The response to this has been a mixture of enthusiasm and uneasiness. No one wants to have a phone conversation with an automated digital assistant, but at the same time it would not hurt to have computers schedule appointments on our behalf. It is not exactly work that anyone enjoys; I wouldn't miss having to take time out of my day to make a several-minute phone call to schedule an oil change.

The uneasiness seems to derive from the sense that this development takes us one step further from other people. When we let a computer write our emails for us, it means that we are automating away our connections to other human beings.

And that is, in a sense, true, at the same time that I doubt many people will allow Gmail to autocomplete the messages they send their loved ones. Rather, this advanced form of autocomplete is likely to help us with our work emails, the messages we have to send one another in the course of a busy day at the office—which will free us up to do any number of other things that are more essential and valuable. It means less time spent writing a message to accompany a document we are attaching for a colleague, and more time spent perfecting the documents our colleagues expect us to send to them.

Email has become so familiar to us, it is easy to forget what a relatively recent innovation it is. It wasn't very long ago that no one, anywhere, spent any of their time writing electronic messages to others; the technology had not been developed yet. And when it came into being, it meant, for many people, a certain ease with communication at the same time that it became an obligation—another form of work we had to do in the course of our jobs. In this case, the thing that has been automated is something that only recently began to place a burden on us.

This is one way in which automation is helping to make the modern world more sustainable, more amenable to those of us who live in it. It simplifies the work that isn't especially important, so that we can do the things that are important—freeing us up to do the things that matter to us. The most powerful AI system in the world cannot write a confessional email to an old high school friend—something that email is still abundantly useful for.

THE JOHN HENRY MODEL

I often think that our perception of how technology influences work is caught in a John Henry model—meaning that we think of how technology comes to supplant human laborers as something like what became of the folk hero John Henry. When a steam engine was brought to his worksite, and all the other railroad workers saw it as their replacement, he challenged it to a race; he and the steam engine competed to see which of them could hammer their way through the mountain faster. Against the odds, John Henry won, only to die of exhaustion immediately after, his hammer still in his hand.

A human being might excel at a job, and even be a kind of superman—like John Henry—but eventually, according to this model, a machine will be brought in to replace that human being. The capable human worker will be removed from their job, and will perhaps even, like John Henry, die. The result will be, to some degree, tragic. It entails a demonstrable loss, like the death of the story's hero.

Like him, we can try to outperform a machine, and we may even, like him, succeed momentarily, but we are not likely to survive the contest; we are doomed to become mere legends as the work we do is automated and we are rendered obsolete.

But it doesn't have to work like that. Or it does—but there is more to the story. After the death of John Henry is the loss of a form of labor for the people who were swinging hammers to dig tunnels for the railroads. As was inevitable, other forms of work came to replace the dumb labor that was just asking to be automated.

I admit that this version of the story would not make for a very good folktale, let alone song—but John Henry did not have to challenge the steam drill to a test of strength and capability. He could instead have gone into a different line of work, one where his emotional intelligence and capacity to think critically would have served him. He didn't have to try to do the same work as a machine, and do it better; he could have sidestepped that booby trap and taken up a different sort of work altogether.

It is not a heroic narrative, and so there are no songs written about the one who saw the steam drill and, rather than challenge it to a contest, left in order to make a living some other way. But that is the more tenable option, and it is one we would do well to be mindful of as we watch AI subsume so much of the work we currently do.

THE NEED FOR SUSTAINABILITY

As we see our world change, and change again, we should pressure those who are responsible for changing it to have sustainability in mind at all times. I mention it again because it is not something we have been very good with, so far.

An article by Evan Selinger, a philosophy professor at the Rochester Institute of Technology, asks, "Will Tech Companies Ever Take Ethics Seriously?"

According to Selinger, they have not done so in the past. He lists some of the downsides to popular developments like social media, with their effects on us that include "attachment, dependence, vulnerability, lock-in, and a sense of being exploited and of that exploitation being validated." Selinger does not discuss sustainability per se, but everything he has to say on this subjects relates to sustainability. He acknowledges the frequent comparison between tech companies and tobacco companies; he downplays that comparison, but it only highlights the plain fact that the tobacco company model was not a sustainable one. Big tobacco sought to addict whole generations of people to products that were likely to harm or even kill them. Tobacco companies are still around, but they were bound to suffer as the public learned more about the harm that cigarettes caused. To make tech companies behave more ethically is to make them behave more sustainably; the two things go hand-in-hand.

It is neither ethical nor sustainable, for example, for tech companies to—in Selinger's words—carry out an "agenda of weaponizing design choices so that the machinery is optimized to extract maximum personal information from tech users." Citizens and legislators have had too little say, he goes on to argue, in the design of the technologies they use. As a result, they are designed without them in mind, and thus without sustainability in mind. And there has been "a perfect storm of neglect running from policymakers through CEOs alike."

One of the remedies Selinger has to prescribe is an increased emphasis on ethical education, ensuring that programmers and engineers are taught design ethics as they learn to create the technologies that influence many aspects of our lives. "I believe," he explains, "that conceptual tools, like carefully crafted and smartly interpreted thought experiments, can help people think in novel and creative ways, much like the most challenging quality fiction, film, and fine art do." It is not hard to imagine how such an education can be made supplemental to the upskilling that will keep people current with developments in their fields.[56]

We should implement this education in ethics not only because it is the right thing to do. It is hard to get private companies to implement changes on that basis alone; for the sake of their survival, they tend to be more interested in staying profitable than they are in doing the right thing. Indeed, taking ethical concerns seriously is a matter of survival in the long term; a company can find success while cutting corners and crushing people who stand in its way. But it will only be a matter of time before the pendulum swings the other way, and whatever has been built up is put at risk. Emphasizing sustainability is not only in the best interests of individuals; it is the best thing a company can do for itself.

THE PROBLEM OF CORRUPTION

The groundbreaking and game-changing technologies of AI and data collection will alter things dramatically. In order to ensure we are prepared for them, we must attend to the health of our longstanding institutions, our structures of government. The problems that press upon us at this moment are old ones, made more dire by impending surges in technology.

Corruption of politicians has been a problem for as long as there have been politicians. The Romans had corrupt politicians. America's Gilded Age was one in which corruption was the order of the day, and there were no computers then.

Now we face a possible future in which corruption meets artificial intelligence, in which, if we do not address the problem of corruption, we face being stuck with it forever.

We have seen, in the debate over gun control and the Second Amendment, how money can influence a public debate and the people we count on to act on our behalf. Gun rights groups, notably the National Rifle Association, pay

---

56 Evan Selinger. "Will Tech Companies Ever Take Ethics Seriously?" *Medium.* April 9, 2018. *https://medium.com/s/story/will-tech-companies-ever-take-ethics-seriously-35d991f9f839* (accessed May 9, 2018).

politicians to represent their interests, and make it nearly impossible to impose restrictions on access to guns. Options for increased public safety like arming teachers are on the table, while measures like banning assault-style weapons are unheard of. It is, by now, a familiar and deeply frustrating story.

If we do not do something about the influence of money and those who have enormous sums of it on our politicians, we can expect the same scenario to play out with AI. We may call for the use of this new technology to be regulated, for protections to be put in place that will preserve us from the harm that AI can do to our individual lives and social fabric. But if our politicians are receiving massive campaign donations from the likes of Facebook and Google, it will be virtually impossible for us to accomplish any such thing. The sums of money these companies have to dole out to our representatives is far beyond anything the NRA has at its disposal. Any politician who wants to receive campaign donations from the likes of these companies will know perfectly well that regulating their technologies is forbidden. This tendency was on display at Mark Zuckerberg's hearing before the Senate, the subtext of which, for too many of the participants, was that they were willing to overlook certain missteps by Facebook and forego regulation—perhaps, we are left to imagine, in return for something.

If we do not do something to address this kind of thing soon, and address as well the influence of digital technology on our political processes, we might well find ourselves trapped. We are still only beginning to reckon with the influence of big data and social media on our democracy. The effort to uncover this is as fraught as anything, with one of our two political parties—the dominant one, which seems to have benefited most—taking little to no interest in learning anything about it.

That influence is set only to increase, as systems that work against our interest are powered using AI and data collection. The machines we have made can already conjecture our interests and desires, based on what little information we provide them, often with startling accuracy. They can influence the decisions we make—not only concerning what products to buy, but whom to vote for.

They will only get better at doing this. They will work better and faster, prying us from what little power we have as individuals, and rendering us essentially helpless. Millions of people were taken aback to learn the role that Facebook played in influencing the 2016 US presidential election. We are only beginning to reckon with it, but as we do, we must ask what comes after it, and what rules we establish for preventing its more insidious influence on us.

One possible and quite likely future is one in which machine learning systems collect information on the choices we make, politically, and our feelings about certain issues and questions, and hand the sum of that information to psychologists, who can use it to determine what drives our behaviors and preferences, and leverage it against our best interests. If, for the sake of argument, I like watching short, violent films on YouTube (I don't), then a political campaign that knows that about me can arrange to have me served with more short, violent films, each one preceded by ads for their candidate. They would thus ensure that I receive the message they want to send, without my knowing they are doing this. They could craft messages that appeal perfectly to my tastes, which they have determined by monitoring the media I prefer. It is a way of taking a mass of people and, on an individual, completely automated basis, diverting their attention into ever-narrowing channels and ensuring their attention does not stray from them.

This is a dangerous possibility; it is a way of using technology against the individual, and politically hamstringing great masses of people. I say this not as a diehard political activist, but as someone who has worked in technology, who has paid attention, and who understands the stakes involved.

We have every reason to regulate the use and development of AI. Its technology can be used for our benefit or against our best interests; it doesn't have to be a means for swaying our opinions and political leanings so that we work against our own interests. It can be used, instead, to make education more personalized and effective, so that our children have completely personalized courses of study at all levels, rather than programs that are meant to suit a vast number of people who have little in common with one another.

As Ben Y. Zhao, Professor of Computer Science at the University of Chicago, has stated, the problem we face in the new technologies is probably not an immanently catastrophic one. We miss the point of this technology if the dangers we anticipate are limited to the development of a vast military computer, like Skynet from *The Terminator*. "My simple intuition," he explains,

> says AI regulation is a good idea. ML experts are pushing hard to solve problems that would a) accelerate how fast models learn, and b) help models self-improve by fixing problems that produce suboptimal performance w.r.t. specific metrics. Combine the two, and it seems like you have all the makings of a runaway train. From a conservative standpoint, regulation makes a lot of sense, because this is a problem that in the worst case, has world-ending implications. And if we want to have any hope of doing it "right," we need to give it time. The FDA, FCC, or any of the other regulatory agencies (if this is indeed an apt analogy), all took a long time to settle down into what they are today. Any attempt to regulate AI would require significant effort to educate some policy makers, and much more time to come up with some understanding of what "regulation" even means in the world of AI.

There are arguments against regulating AI. There are those who say it is too early to know how to regulate it properly, or that we risk stifling development of new technology in the United States, leaving it to the Chinese, Russians, or North Koreans to surpass us and learn how to harness its power at our expense. But, Zhao explains,

> I've been somewhat surprised by how dismissive some of the opposing arguments have been. The general answer has been "we are so far away from world ending AI, e.g. Skynet, and there are much more important problems today in the world." But I find that argument unconvincing. The security community has seen this mistake made over and over for decades. Security considerations/mechanisms cannot be added after the fact. Yet system builders routinely ignore this, and build systems with critical design flaws...So if it requires some

overabundance of cautionary measures, it's probably worth it. The argument of "we have other, more important problems" fails, because it assumes a level of rationality and liquidity of resources that does not exist. Congress will not become more productive on climate change because it freed up resources from regulating AI.

Zhao goes on to explain that he is far less worried about cataclysmic problems, like the accidental invention of a self-aware military network that decides the human race is obsolete, than he is about old-fashioned problems, like human error—like people making small mistakes that have serious implications. He warns against "unpredictable outcomes with 'bugs' that are undetectable by users or engineers, simply because of how opaque they are." It may not be the evil genius with an army of attack robots, powered by AI, that we need to worry about. The real threat may lie with the legion of computer engineers who are prone to making mistakes that threaten to have implications even they cannot predict.[57]

Perhaps the most effective way to ensure the sustainability of things as they are is to establish bulwarks against small mistakes having vastly destructive effects on us. We should not forget that regulations are how we protect ourselves against the negligence or bad intentions of others, but also their well-meaning projects that happen to cut corners at the expense of our well-being.

We have seen this before, after all; there are lessons we ought to have learned by now. By the late 1980s, it was clear that chlorofluorocarbons (CFCs) were contributing to the depletion of the ozone layer. The chemicals were pouring out of refrigerators, air conditioners, and aerosol cans. Holes in the ozone layer were growing, accelerating the melting of sea ice and increasing skin cancer rates. And so, in 1987, nations the world over signed the Montreal Protocol, a global agreement to limit the production and consumption of substances that deplete the ozone layer. According to the

57 Ben Y. Zhao. "Should Artificial Intelligence Be Regulated?" *Forbes.* August 31, 2017. *https://www.forbes.com/sites/quora/2017/08/31/should-artificial-intelligence-be-regulated/#5228f95b331d* (accessed May 21, 2018).

US Department of State, "Full implementation of the Montreal Protocol is expected to result in avoidance of more than 280 million cases of skin cancer, approximately 1.6 million skin cancer deaths, and more than 45 million cases of cataracts in the United States alone by the end of the century, with even greater benefits worldwide."[58]

Regulations can work. They are the only protections we have, in many cases, against the excesses of industry and self-serving greed. There is no excuse for our taking no action to preserve ourselves from the side effects of today's innovations, and it is of grave concern that the tendency, lately, has been to roll back regulations that are currently in place, with the reversal of policy on net neutrality, to take one enormously consequential example.

We must take seriously the need to regulate the innovations that will influence our lives—because the ones whose companies are regulated, and, in some cases, the regulators themselves, will fight the new rules with everything they have. Writing in The Baffler, Aaron Timms predicts a rash of "regulatory wars" and a concerted effort to blunt the effects of regulation, "in which public outrage and demands for reform eventually soften and industry works to dilute proposed reforms once public attention has drifted elsewhere." Dissecting some of the language used by Facebook CEO Mark Zuckerberg at his now-famous appearance before Congress, Timms writes, "'Unexpected consequences,' 'well-crafted': These are the code words that signal not the advent of a new era of robust government oversight, but the start of the anti-regulatory resistance."[59]

If regulations were not effective and worthwhile, they would hardly be worth resisting or preempting in this way. It is up to us to ensure that pressure is applied to legislators, and that we keep it up. Our very well-being depends upon it.

---

58 "The Montreal Protocol on Substances That Deplete the Ozone Layer."
US Department of State. https://www.state.gov/e/oes/eqt/chemicalpollution/83007.htm (accessed May 30, 2018).

59 Aaron Timms. "Unexpected Consequences." *The Baffler.* April 17, 2018.
https://thebaffler.com/latest/unexpected-consequences-timms (accessed May 30, 2018).

TECHNOLOGY AND INCLUSIVITY

As I was writing this chapter I saw a talk, hosted by MIT, on human-machine interaction. One of the panelists, Kat Holmes, started her own business after working at companies like Microsoft and Google, with a focus on inclusion. Her company, Kata, endeavors to promote inclusion in tech and elsewhere.[60]

What does "inclusion" mean, in this context? On her blog, she poses exactly that question, asking, "What does inclusion actually mean—especially when it's so feverishly applied to broad areas of society?" She makes her way toward answering that question by discussing inclusion's opposite: exclusion. We have all, she explains, been excluded from a group or an experience. "Every choice we make as designers," she writes, "determines who can use an environment or product. The mismatches that we create in the process are the building blocks of exclusion. From the stairs at the entrance of a building to the two-handed design of a video game controller, our solutions clearly signal who does and doesn't belong." And so her work involves promoting inclusion in a culture where inclusion is not quite a priority. As she explained at the MIT panel, more than a billion and a half people in the world have disabilities—and so this is in no way an abstract or detached consideration; this is something that affects the lives of many.

If we are to shape a world that is equable, and sustainably so, we must ensure that it is inclusive—that as many people have access to it as possible. We must do this in the name of sustainability, and for the overall health of the systems we inhabit. We all stand to benefit from as many people as possible having access to the technologies we use.

And many of us do benefit from this consideration already, even if we are not conscious of that fact. The technologies we use on a daily, even hourly, basis are only accessible to us because their designers had inclusion—of us—in mind.

---

60 Town Hall Seattle. "Human-Machine Interfaces & the Future of Interaction." YouTube. *https://www.youtube.com/watch?v=O8QV1qs3mrc* (accessed May 22, 2018).

There is much to be said for the design of the typical computer, for the way it deploys the familiar layout of a typewriter keyboard, and the organizational tools of items within windows that can be moved from window to window. These are simple concepts. They do not take long to understand and learn to use. It was not always like this; in the age of the Commodore 64, not nearly as many people had computers as we see now. This is in part because as the years have gone by, computers have become more inclusive.

Computers are not perfectly designed to be user-friendly; they are not equally welcoming to everyone. The standard laptop screen does not necessarily serve the needs of the visually impaired. If I lost my hands in a terrible lawncare accident, I would have to find an alternative to using my keyboard. I don't know, off the top of my head, what that alternative would be—which might say something about what more there is to do in the way of promoting inclusion.

But imagine how more exclusive computers would be if, instead of using typewriter-style keyboards, all computer input were done using piano keyboards—so that anyone who wanted to use a computer had to first learn the rudiments of playing the piano.

It is hard to imagine, because developers of this technology chose a different path. But there was a time when the use of computers was not nearly as inclusive as it is now, when to use a computer meant inserting punch cards into a giant device, rather than pressing keys with letters and numbers printed on them. When computers entered the next stage in their long lifecycle, they became more inclusive. The iPhone was another step in that direction; a child can learn to use its interface in a matter of minutes.

This brings us back to the regulatory movement of the 1970s that reshaped our public spaces so that they are accessible to those who use wheelchairs; every public building we enter has been built to accommodate the disabled. It is hard to imagine things being otherwise, but not long ago, they were. It is hard to look at the exclusion that preceded those accessibility regulations as anything other than cruel; so it is with the world we are watching come into being, and the ways we may unwittingly deny certain people access to them.

For this reason, we must invest in individualized, high-quality education and the infrastructure it requires, so that the greatest number of people can thrive in the twenty-first century.

Inclusion is something we should have in mind as we watch our working lives undergo their revolution, if only because with the adoption of AI they are bound to become somewhat less inclusive. On her blog, Holmes writes about the encounter between a potential user and the piece of technology that excludes them: "In these moments, many people are more likely to blame themselves than the object. They might feel left behind and wonder why technology changes so much faster than they do. Moreover, it's often unclear who's responsible for fixing that exclusion."[61]

She is addressing the situation that the blind may find themselves in when faced with a computer monitor. But it could just as easily be a description of the situation project managers find themselves in when they are laid off from work, thanks to the adoption of an AI program that does the same work better and faster than any human being. The potential issues are the same: the alienated users blaming themselves; the feeling of being left behind; not knowing who can or should fix the problem, or even where the problem lies, exactly.

Inclusion should not be treated as something abstract, by anyone—for, in an instant, we can find ourselves excluded from the use of technology we once found it easy to work with. It isn't a matter, necessarily, of going blind or having our fingers removed by a rogue lawnmower. It is far more likely to be the result of technology shifting forward suddenly in a way that makes it harder for us to use it, and easier for us to be used by it.

THE REACH OF SUSTAINABILITY

As is the case so many dimensions of this subject matter, writing a chapter about sustainability has been like unfolding a vast fabric of ideas; one

---

61 Kat Holmes. "What We're Leaving Out of the Discussion Around Inclusive Design." April 26, 2018. *https://blog.kata.design* (accessed May 22, 2018).

innovation speaks to another, which leads inevitably to something else.

This makes sense; to take sustainability seriously, and consider it a goal, means approaching the Fourth Industrial Revolution and its aftermath from many different angles.

This chapter could go on indefinitely. But if we take nothing else from this whole discussion, it should be that sustainability is not a concern to be left only to environmentalists.

There are three primary legs, if you will, to sustainability: social, economic, and environmental. For the sake of this book, I have focused on the social and economic legs of this concern, as the goal is to create a bearable and equable world. I don't mean to suggest a lack of concern for environmental sustainability by not paying it much attention here; rather, I believe that because environmental sustainability gets so much (deserved) attention, we tend to overlook those other kinds of sustainability that matter just as much.

Sustainability is a principle that we must take into consideration everywhere we turn—which is no small thing, in a world in which every new product is made to grow obsolete in a couple of years, thanks to swift advances in technology.

We must work to create a world that can last, one that isn't bound to be cast aside by the next generation of people. To be attuned to sustainability is one way to achieve exactly that.

CHAPTER SIX:

Reputation Will Drive Engagement

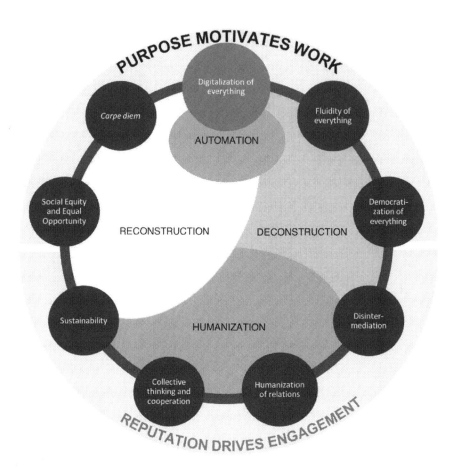

Figure 10. Trends
Source: CollectiveBrains

AS WE SEE IN FIGURE 10, our recurring Trends chart, the increased force of our reputations is equally important to how purpose will come to motivate our work more and more. In the new world that is rapidly replacing the old one, reputation will drive our engagement with our workplaces, with each other, and with the labor that we perform.

The reasons for the increased importance of a worker's reputation is plain; as more of our work becomes virtual and remote, people will rely on our reputations more than ever in order to know us.

In 2011, the Institute for the Future, a research group that works to predict changes to workplaces and the business ecosystem, laid out the ten most important skills to be put to use in the workplace of the imminent future. Among these, they included virtual collaboration: "the ability to work productively, drive engagement, [and] demonstrate presence as a member of a virtual team." They elaborated, in their *Future Work Skills 2020* report, by describing this virtual collaboration, and how it is likely to be manifested:

> Connective technologies make it easier than ever to work, share ideas and be productive despite physical separation. But the virtual work environment also demands a new set of competencies. As a leader of a virtual team, individuals need to develop strategies for engaging and motivating a dispersed group…A community that offers "ambient sociability" can help overcome isolation that comes from lack of access to a central, social workplace. This could be a physical coworking space, but it could also be virtual…Online streams created by micro blogging and social networking sites can serve as virtual water coolers, providing a sense of camaraderie and enabling employees to

demonstrate presence.[62]

When the work we do is carried out in a virtual space inhabited by others, we must adapt our communication skills, and rethink how we go about being among coworkers. A compelling sense of purpose will bring us to the workplace, and the workplace itself will be unlike what we are accustomed to.

It will be one where our reputations have a far greater significance than they currently do. Our reputations are important to us now; they always have been. But when we report to a virtual space in order to work, rather than travel someplace physically, then the ways in which we are perceived by others will be very different. Physical appearance will be mostly irrelevant, perhaps even completely so. We will have, arguably, more control over how we present ourselves to others; we will be far more able to edit our appearances, because the ways in which we communicate will be mostly virtual.

Our interactions with one another are likely, furthermore, to be documented and analyzed by artificial intelligence. We will have a constant, perfect assistant, a go-between who will track and record what we say to one another, which will keep us on-task and keep us informed as to what our colleagues are doing and the progress they are making toward our shared objectives. The work we do will be tracked and recorded, automatically, so as to enhance our successes.

One result of this is that our reputations will be quantifiable. The good work we do will contribute to an ongoing account of our working lives—a well-sourced and meticulously constructed reputation. We will grow ever more answerable to a meticulous account of what we have accomplished, and how we may have fallen short.

The effect of our work on our reputation will be more direct than ever. And so, with the rise of collective intelligence will come a change in our roles as individuals in the workplace. Some of the mystery will be lost; people will have a much easier way to learn who we are and what we have done, and

---

62 Institute for the Future for the University of Phoenix Research Institute. *Future Work Skills 2020*. http://www.iftf.org/uploads/media/SR-1382A_UPRI_future_ work_skills_sm.pdf (accessed April 23, 2018).

will not have to rely on the ways in which we choose to represent ourselves; conversely, it will not be up to us to remind one another of what we have accomplished and where we have been—our work will speak for itself with an amplified voice.

Our reputations, which already influence how we fare on the job market and how we are perceived in the workplace, will be far more definite, far more precise. We have every reason to welcome this change. It means taking something that is indefinite, unreliable, and hard to control, and making it into something we can rely on to reflect our strong performances and help make us successful.

STARS ARE WORTH MORE THAN MONEY

As with so many of the oncoming changes to the way we work, this one is already, in some ways, visible to us. Reputation has long been emerging as the primary currency for many industries and workplaces.

Websites like Yelp have seen to it that restaurants and other businesses must stay on their toes if they want to continue to attract customers; an excess of bad reviews can keep potential new patrons at bay, which means a diminished revenue stream, or—in many cases—the dissolution of a business altogether. Stars can be more important than cash; ask anyone who owns a small business.

No one understands this better, perhaps, than those who drive for Uber. They are rated on a five-star scale every time they drop off a passenger at their destination—something they do over and over again throughout a workday, making them accountable to a vast array of complete strangers. Swerving too much, being uncongenial to riders, having a car that isn't as clean as expected, playing the wrong music or no music, or simply failing to meet the expectations of an individual passenger, can have disastrous results, if it leads someone to give the driver a low rating. It was reported in 2015 that if a driver's average rating dropped below 4.6, they were prone to being removed from Uber altogether.[63] This is perhaps the most direct case of the cause-and-effect dynamic in which one's livelihood depends wholly on how one's performance is judged in aggregate.

Up to now, information workers have been insulated from this way of working, from such accountability to the people they work for and with. But this dynamic is coming to the modern workplace; it will arrive before we know it.

That may sound daunting, even alienating; no one relishes being evaluated, and the prospect of being evaluated more often by more people than we are currently accountable does not exactly sound like a delightful picnic. But there is a great deal of good that can and will come from this, and the picture isn't really as grim as it may appear at first glance. For one thing, most people's jobs are nothing like that of the Uber or Lyft driver; being accountable to others does not mean having to rely on the goodwill and fair evaluation of fifty or more people per day. Most of us work with far fewer people than that, and they know us for months or years at a time. The impressions we give them will accrue over time; we will have many opportunities to impress them and boost our ratings.

Performance evaluation will not be a concern once or twice a year, but constantly, and management will have far more metrics to rely on as they go about it. Reputations will come to hold greater sway over whether someone is considered hirable by a given company. They will be quantified, based on precise metrics.

To a certain extent, this is nothing new; it is merely an old thing in a new and better form. People are already evaluated based on their reputations. If you are notorious in your particular industry, for being a tyrant, or a stubborn loner who takes credit for everyone else's work, but does nothing for himself, then no one will want to work with you. You will be shut out.

---

63 James Cook. "Uber's internal charts show how its driver-rating system actually works." *Business Insider*. February 11, 2015. *https://www.businessinsider.com/leaked-charts-show-how-ubers-driver-rating-system-works-2015-2* (accessed May 22, 2018).

Or—what is worse—you might have this reputation and thrive in your field despite it. Everyone might know you are impossible to work with, even detrimental to the mental health of those who surround you, but be made to work with you despite the harm you cause on a daily basis. Despite how your reputation precedes you, it does not take a definite or reliable form; because reputations are currently amorphous composites of so many different impressions of you, it is hard to gain a foothold and take some sort of action to phase you out and improve the workplace.

Reputations are unreliable things, as it stands now. They can hardly be relied on for precise reflections of the work one has done or what one is capable of. They aggregate from rumors, potentially unreliable testimonies, and workplace successes that might well be incidental to the presence of the person in question. It is about time we changed this.

THE REPUTATION-BASED WORKPLACE

Reputations will only grow more important with time, as we rely on them to help us secure one job after another; soon we will not work in quite the way we are accustomed to. Job security as we have known it will be a thing of the past, if it isn't already; think of the situation of the Uber driver, versus that of the taxi driver. The former can be out of a job in a day, if enough rides go poorly; the latter could have secured access to a taxi and been in business indefinitely. All of our jobs will soon go the way of the traditional taxi driver; we will have steady work, but it will come to us on a project-by-project basis.

At the moment, it can seem like a steep demotion, to go from having great job security as a taxi driver to suddenly driving for Uber. But the situation of those drivers is not likely to remain quite what it is for long. As it stands now, a disaffected Uber driver can abandon the service in favor of Lyft. But imagine if there were even more options than that—if there were as many such companies to drive for as there currently are taxi services in an urban center, all of them competing with one another for drivers. In that case, reputation would not be a liability, but an asset. Job security would be something undesirable; signing a three-year contract with one company would be limiting. A driver could hop from one company to another, throughout a given week, working most often for those companies that offer the best fares or shares of the profits.

This is something more like what we have to look forward to, as reputations increase in importance, and become more definite and quantifiable. The white-collar workplace will be more reputation-based, but we will not be nailed down to a specific workplace for long. We will have many options to choose from. This is already the case for many workers, such as those in technology, whose expertise is in high demand and who can leap from job to job. Rather than work for one company, qualified experts work for many companies, in advisory roles. They are not tied down to one workplace; they can offer their services to whomever they want.

We can expect to benefit from a similar work dynamic, in which we will be far more in control of our own destinies than we are now, as we will have more freedom to choose where we direct our precious time and resources. Our reputations will be the vessels that take us from one short-term job to another, as we stitch them together out of our work experience and professional accomplishments.

BULLIES

It is about time we shook up the traditional workplace. Modern life, in so many ways, is vastly different from the way people lived just several decades ago. But workplaces have, by and large, not changed at all.

As Anne-Marie Slaughter wrote in a *New York Times* editorial, in 2015, "The people who can compete and succeed in this culture are an ever-narrower slice of American society: largely young people who are healthy, and wealthy enough not to have to care for family members." In her article, Slaughter focuses on the plight of women who want to offer their talents and abilities to the workplace, but find they cannot do it without sacrificing the rest of their lives; if they have children, their careers suffer, thanks to stringent workplace requirements and demands on their time. As Slaughter wrote, "This looks like a 'women's problem,' but it's not. It's a work problem—the problem of an antiquated and broken system." As one woman she interviewed put it, 'I haven't yet been presented with a shred of reasonable justification for insisting my job requires me to be sitting in this fixed, 15 sq foot room, 20 miles from my home.'"[64]

The problem isn't only that workplaces have not changed to keep up with a changing workforce and the ever-shifting nature of the work we do. Workplace culture has remained in place, as well, with all of the unfortunate side effects of gathering many people in one place, who have little to nothing in common with one another, and expecting them to remain there for eight hours at a time. If they don't do this, they risk losing their income and healthcare; they keep coming back because they have no choice but to do so.

This is a setting where bullies thrive. It is where those who are productive, even brilliantly so, but who are also quiet and unassuming in person, tend to be overshadowed by those who accomplish little but speak loudly about themselves, or otherwise know how to navigate the office power structure and get what they want.

And bullies do, in fact, do very well at our current workplaces. The Workplace Bullying Institute reported in 2017 that 61 percent of Americans are "aware of abusive conduct in the workplace." 19 percent of employees are bullied, 61 percent of bullies are bosses—and, "In the absence of legal prohibitions against it, employers are failing to take responsibility for its prevention and correction."[65]

That impossible boss you had once—or have now—who made you dread going to work in the morning, turned your colleagues against one another, and whose occasional absence from the workplace changed the atmosphere

---

64 Anne-Marie Slaughter. "A Toxic Work World." *The New York Times.* September 18, 2015. *https://www.nytimes.com/2015/09/20/opinion/sunday/a-toxic-work-world.html* (accessed May 22, 2018).

65 Gary Namie. "2017 WBI U.S. Workplace Bullying Survey." *Workplace Bullying Institute.* June 2017. *http://www.workplacebullying.org/wbiresearch/wbi-2017-survey/* (accessed May 30, 2018).

of the place completely, for the far, far better, was not an isolated case. The problem of workplace bullying is widespread, and it is serious.

For this and many other reasons, intuition tells us—and, more importantly, the data tell us—that people are unhappy at work. Not only are they not happy, they are disengaged, and that these things overlap is no coincidence.

Gallup found in 2017 that 85 percent of employees were not engaged at work, with 18 percent described themselves as actively disengaged and 67 percent as simply "not engaged"—meaning, "They give you their time, but not their best effort nor their best ideas. They likely come to work wanting to make a difference—but nobody has ever asked them to use their strengths to make the organization better."[66] The inefficiency that results from this, also according to Gallup, can cost a company $3,400 for every $10,000 of an employee's salary. And so a disengaged employee who makes $70,000 may cost the company they work for an additional $23,800 per year.

It is for this reason that Amazon offers to pay its fulfillment center employees $5,000 to quit working for Amazon and not come back. It sounds like an outlandish, boneheaded thing to do. But we should not see this tactic as evidence only of just how much money and resources Amazon has at its disposal. It turns out that, in the long run, it is less expensive to entice disengaged people to leave with money than it is to pay them to stay.[67]

Disengagement at work means unhappiness at work, which often means unhappiness with life overall; how could it not, when so many of us spend so much of our time at our workplaces?

A study in 2014 by Conference Board, a nonprofit research group, found that 52.3 percent of Americans were unhappy at work. Happiness at work has decreased since the survey began in 1987. The only aspects of the survey

---

66 Jim Harter. "Dismal Employee Engagement Is a Sign of Global Mismanagement." *Gallup*. December 20, 2017. *http://news.gallup.com/opinion/gallup/224012/dismal-employee-engagement-sign-global-mismanagement.aspx* (accessed May 30. 2018).

67 Ruth Umoh. "Why Amazon Pays Employees $5,000 to Quit." *MSN*. May 21, 2018. *https://www.msn.com/en-us/money/companies/why-amazon-pays-employees-dollar5000-to-quit/ar-AAxAqrT* (accessed May 30, 2018).

where there have been gains in happiness have to do with work environment, which the study's authors chalk up to so many workers telecommuting from home—meaning that people are only happier at work than they used to be because some of them do not have to physically be there.[68]

It should come as no surprise that people who are able to leave their workplaces are, by and large, doing so—whether it is because the company is paying them to go, because they are in search of better, more fulfilling work elsewhere, or because they can manage on their own, working on a contract-by-contract basis and not having to answer to a bully or a stagnant workplace culture. It is only a matter of time before we flee such toxic spaces en masse in favor of something better.

EDUCATION AT WORK

This new way of moving from job to job, and having careers that look like patchwork quilts, will make it far easier for workers to continue to educate themselves, to prepare themselves for each upcoming job by undertaking a brief and relevant course of study. And this ongoing education will have great, positive effects on our reputations; potential employers will know precisely what we are capable of because our reputations will reflect how we have prepared ourselves for the work ahead.

Signs indicate that it will be up to companies themselves to provide the education employees will need. As Rachel Illingworth has written, for the consulting company Appirio,

> To close the skills gap and compete for today's top talent, organizations need to provide opportunities for growth and learning. Glassdoor estimates that 60 percent of millennials consider the most attractive job perk to be growth opportunities. By creating a collaborative learning environment, employees will feel more fulfilled and engaged, and can

---

68 Susan Adams. "Most Americans Are Unhappy at Work." *Forbes.* June 20, 2014. *https://www.forbes.com/sites/susanadams/2014/06/20/most-americans-are-unhappy-at-work/* (accessed June 7, 2018).

gain important skills to excel in their jobs.

And so just as work will soon be done, by and large, collaboratively, Illingworth projects that learning will be undertaken in the same way. Just as our workplaces will change, so will the way we are educated, as we have discussed previously.

Illingworth goes on to cite the faucet manufacturer Moen, which hired Appirio to help address their loss of personnel at certain levels of the company. Appirio implemented a learning and development plan for Moen's field service and middle-management workers, plugging that particular hole by working to foster an atmosphere of continued education.[69]

In this same way, we can expect workers of every stripe to be educated at their workplaces, so that they can be more effective there. And as with so many of the changes that lie ahead, this one does not mean the invention of something altogether new. Education already takes place at the workplace, only in a seriously inefficient and haphazard fashion. New hires arrive at the workplace with degrees in hand, but often with little to no familiarity with the tasks they will in fact carry out on a day-to-day basis. And so they have to learn as they go, by taking up the time of supervisors or colleagues, or simply fumbling through their early days on the job, slowly figuring things out on their own. A report from *Training* magazine indicates that in 2007 companies spent an average of $1,200 per year training each of its employees.[70] Total spending by US companies in 2015 amounted to more than $70 billion.[71]

Solutions to this are already emerging. As Yoav Vilner writes in *Inc.*, one low-cost means for speeding up this process is the use of employee

---

69 Rachel Illingworth. "In a World of Skills Gaps, Moen Prioritizes Development and Learning." *Appirio*. September 5, 2017. *https://hub.appirio.com/customer-stories/in-a-world-of-skills-gaps-moen-prioritizes-development-and-learning* (June 8, 2018).

70 "The True Cost of Hiring a New Employee." *Undercover Recruiter*. *https://theundercoverrecruiter.com/true-cost-hiring-new-employee/* (accessed June 8, 2018).

71 Yoav Vilner. "3 Ways to Cut Employee Onboarding and Training Costs." *Inc.* *https://www.inc.com/yoav-vilner/3-ways-to-cut-employee-onboarding-and-training-costs.html* (accessed June 8, 2018).

apps, which, "also known as internal communications apps, are branded smartphone apps that employees use to stay updated with company news, notifications, courses, training and surveys." He cites Slack as an app that has managed to keep workers engaged with one another, keeping them in constant communication, which can facilitate on-the-job learning. Connect-eam is another app that "allow[s] for employees near and far to orient to a new workplace by reading training material and then testing their knowl-edge." A relatively low-tech approach to on-the-job training that Vilner cites is group training, which serves the purpose of on-the-job education at the same time that it builds comradery among employees.[72]

As this kind of ongoing education becomes more pervasive, and more effective, it will be more readily quantifiable; having undertaken a brief course of study will have a direct, positive effect on one's reputation. This will become easier and more effective as reputations become more definite, and as readily accessible as our resumes, only more authoritative and reliable.

THE REPUTATIONS WE SEE NOW

Efforts have been made, already, to make reputations more quantifiable and accessible. LinkedIn is perhaps the most accessible example of a company that has done this.

Everyone knows LinkedIn, even if they don't have a LinkedIn profile; if you have an email address, you have no doubt gotten requests from people you hardly know, asking you to join their LinkedIn networks.

LinkedIn can be useful for someone like myself, who is active in the business world and likes to keep up with others who are similarly engaged. It serves as a valuable forum for ideas, a way to be introduced to business-oriented articles and information. But its usefulness as a way to build a reputation, and to ensure that it is visible, is limited.

The shortcomings of LinkedIn are well-documented. Many have com-plained of its cloying efforts to get people to sign up and return to the site,

---

72 Ibid.

which usually take the form of unwanted emails. Some have questioned its utility. "Most of us," writes Casey Newton of *The Verge*, "don't simply need a service that bombards us daily with professional news and new job prospects. We need a trusted resource that's there for us when we need it—and fades into the background when we don't. LinkedIn is congenitally unable to fade into the background, which is perhaps why so many of us have wished it would just go away. And if it did, who would miss it?"[73] It is a damning assessment of the website, and Newton, as well as others, have more criticisms to heap onto it.

But I like LinkedIn. I use it often. I don't share many of the complaints of its critics; my problem is that it doesn't perform some of its functions nearly as well as it could. I have in mind the limited way it can be used to track and build reputations.

One of the ways in which a user can do that is to have other users offer testimonials, concerning certain skills they claim to have. If I want to switch careers and become a firefighter, I might list skills in my profile that include aiming hoses at burning houses, chopping down doors with axes, and performing CPR on people of all ages. I would benefit from having some well-known fire chiefs sign off on these skills, and so I might solicit their approval of my ability to do these things.

If a fire chief is looking to hire a firefighter, my LinkedIn profile might pique his interest when he saw how well-regarded I was in the firefighting community, and how universally my ability to fight fires was confirmed. Or he might be rightly skeptical of this, because in fact I have never fought a fire in my life, and have no experience saving people or their pets or valuables from burning buildings. In this scenario, I will have gamed the system using LinkedIn and maneuvered myself into a position where I could cause grave harm.

---

73 Casey Newton. "How LinkedIn Failed." *The Verge*. June 14, 2016. *https://www.theverge.com/2016/6/14/11933166/linkedin-microsoft-acquisition-thirsty-email-company* (accessed May 23, 2018).

This is, of course, an extreme example, and I have would have to work fairly hard to trick fire chiefs into approving my claims to having mastered their skills. It would hardly be worth the effort, and might even lead to my arrest.

But if we scale down the absurdity of this example, and posit that an information worker wanted to switch career tracks to a field that's similar enough but which they have no real qualifications for, then that, too, can be done via LinkedIn. I doubt that many people are actually using it to trick hiring managers, at least not successfully, but I do doubt whether many hiring managers place much trust in what they see there.

It can be hard to know, looking at LinkedIn, whom we can trust. Everyone knows not to believe what they see on social media, or what they read online more broadly. This extends to a site like LinkedIn. It is the same trouble faced by a site like RateMyProfessors.com, where college students can go to offer feedback on the performances of professors at any college in the United States, and see what their peers thought of their teaching strategies. So often, though, the reviews are hopelessly biased; it is never clear who is writing the reviews and how well they can be trusted; someone who was given a low grade, rightly, because they performed poorly in the class, might vindictively proclaim on RateMyProfessors that his political science teacher was incompetent.

LinkedIn's system is more sophisticated than this, but it suffers from a similar problem. It has its uses, and I use it often, but it falls short of doing what it is meant to do because we cannot be sure we can trust it. We might check in with it, to see what a profile looks like, but in most cases that is as far as we will take it. There is room for the introduction of more sophisticated resources.

MAKING OUR REPUTATIONS WORK FOR US

We can establish a system whereby our reputations as employees, as coworkers, as citizens of the workplace, are quantifiable according to a star system.

This would be, as we have said, something like the way an Uber or Lyft driver sustains their work with one or the other company—but there would be far more to it than the aggregate votes of disinterested customers. It is far more than a matter of getting every passenger safely from one place to another in a clean vehicle.

It is something more like what many people are already familiar with in the gaming industry—"gaming" in this case meaning video games, rather than gambling. For anyone who is not up to speed with today's video games, they have come a very long way since Pac-Man and Q*bert. The games of today are long-term commitments; they can take hundreds of hours to finish. Players' performances are tracked as they navigate virtual spaces with their in-game personae. They earn points for their accomplishments. Goals are clearly established, and rewards are doled out when they are met.

We can learn an awful lot about how to better incentivize hard work, and how best to quantify progress through a career, from the game designers who have incentivized spending countless hours playing games that simulate the postapocalypse or the old west.

A five-star worker is someone who performs well in myriad ways. They take only as much credit as they have earned, do their fair share of a company's necessary labor, respond to requests swiftly, and do not place unreasonable burdens on others. They are respectful and collegial. They collaborate well and with ease.

We could go on and list a thousand more qualities by which to judge the effectiveness of a fellow worker; the trick is to determine which qualities are most readily quantified, and which of them best represent the overall performance of an individual.

It can be done. It will be done. The reputations we have now will be replaced by those that are more certain, and which are generated in an unbiased fashion, based on performance. It will certainly be better than the way they work currently.

What I am proposing is not the invention of reputations, after all; we all have reputations, as things currently stand. We don't necessarily know what they are. We can hardly be said to control them—and perhaps we shouldn't; if we could decide our own reputations, they would hardly be reliable indications of anything but our opinions of ourselves. But at present, the ways in which people learn about us from afar could hardly be said to be ideal. They include Google searches, which might turn up anything from a fifteen-year-old website you have long since forgotten about, to a misleading preview of a Facebook page that says only that your favorite television show is *The Sopranos*. Someone who wants to learn more about you, without having to talk to you, might look up your LinkedIn page.

But this is far from perfect. And perhaps no way of going about conveying our reputations will be perfect—but we can certainly do better than this. We can establish a system wherein it is plain to see not only what is being said about you, but who is saying it, and how reliable their opinions are. We can take what currently amounts to digital hearsay and turn it into precise data.

This would make it easier to promote people with the right values—people who are willing to collaborate and engage collectively, and who approach their work with an appropriate sense of purpose. We can utterly transform the way we find work and the way we hire workers—and we absolutely should do this, given the changes our working lives are about to undergo.

We can, all the while, abandon so much of the current unpleasantness of job searches. We may never do away with resumes altogether, with the fraught effort on the part of job candidates to represent themselves on one sheet of paper. But we can look forward to a time when we can feel confident that our resumes, sent to hiring managers, will be accompanied by reports on our reputations, which are objective and accurate. We can walk into job interviews knowing what our prospective employers know about us. When, in an interview, we talk about what we have done, the positive things we have brought to companies in the past, we can know for certain that those we are speaking to can back up what we say with concrete information. When seeking to represent themselves in the best light possible, software developers can refer to open source contributions, artists can present their portfolios, architects can rely on the buildings they have designed, and on and on; we can all have similar accomplishments we can demonstrate as readily as this, once they are reified by way of a system that is carefully crafted to present them.

We can, in this way, turn such conversations away from who we are what we do, but how we do what we do and why we do it. Once we can enter such a scene with certain aspects simply understood, we can be free to talk about the aspects of ourselves that matter.

THE REPUTATIONS OF LEADERS

I have expounded already on leadership—on the ways in which the onset of AI and other technologies will eliminate the need for tyrannical or incompetent middle-managers and ring in a new era of leadership. It is worth returning to, as it is another way in which reputation will become supremely important.

For a certain number of workers, it is already the case that they can choose for whom they work, and for what cause. This will soon be the case for many more of them—which means that the evaluation of reputations will work in more than one way. It will not only be a matter of managers choosing their employees based on well-defined track records. A prospective employee will have the opportunity to choose between working for one leader over another, determining things like whether a leader's vision aligns with their own, and how well different leaders treat the people they work with.

HIGH PERFORMANCE TEAM

THE NEW LEADER	Creates trust environment
	Shows caring and compassion
	Great communicator
	Promotes clarity of goals and roles
	Recognize collaboration
	Leverages collective thinking
	Perceived as coach and mentor

Figure 11. The New Leader
Source: CollectiveBrains

We are entering a new era of leadership, and the qualities that make a good leader will only grow more defined. Essential qualities will include the leader's ability to inspire and their resourcefulness. The new leaders will have to pay close attention to the teams they lead, the most notable ones being perfectly attuned to their needs. They will perform the work of managers, but will transcend the role of a mere manager and be a true leader.

As with many other elements of the working world to come, we can look to the better-known aspects of Silicon Valley for faint glimmers of what this will look like. The most notable innovations in digital technology of the last few decades are all closely associated with the leaders who helped bring them about. Everyone knows who brought about the personal computer as we know it, and the iPhone, and the iPod before it. Steve Jobs has been the subject of several films, since his death; he is held up as a paragon of business acumen and technological innovation. But he does not represent the qualities we should expect to see in the leaders of the coming age. He was notoriously difficult to work with; he did not inspire people to do their best work so much as he compelled them to do it. He accomplished an awful lot, but the way he went about it does not represent the leadership of the near future.

There are, perhaps, no such leaders quite yet; every potential such person we have seen so far turns out, upon closer inspection, to have made some regrettable choices at the expense of employees or the public at large. But it is plain to see that a space has been carved out for a new kind of leader. The notable entrepreneurs of Silicon Valley are business executives and public figures; they are leaders in more than simply a business sense. That they fall short of our expectations should not surprise us—but we can look forward to when leaders take their place who are truly deserving of the title. The best leaders will rise to the top; it will be necessary for them to do so, if they have any hope of attracting the best workers and keeping their companies alive. In this realm, as in so many, we can expect to stumble before we stride assuredly forward—but we will do exactly that.

And so, just as employees' reputations must be more definitely quantified and reliably determined and circulated, we must better define what we seek in a leader, and what qualities are most desirable and admirable—so that we can more definitely judge whether we would fit well with those leaders and thrive under them.

There is more to effective, inspiring leadership than simply not being a tyrant. Just as workers will be motivated to work by the purposes they have in mind, leaders will have to lead based on purpose, and have plainly defined goals and values they strive to fulfill.

I, for one, am currently doing exactly that. As I work to get my company off the ground, I have thirteen great people working with me. Only two of them are making any money. And yes, it is true that the rest of them are working with the promise of future equity in the company—but they are also doing it because they believe in what we are working toward, and trust that we collaborate in the name of something that is worthwhile, that offers a sufficient sense of purpose. I am not a perfect leader, but I know that it is incumbent upon me to provide that, in order to attract the best people. And I absolutely believe that I have.

GETTING BACK TO OURSELVES

The new importance of leadership is just one aspect of a broader shift we will see as the Fourth Industrial Revolution takes place. We will come into touch, once again, with what makes us human.

The pendulum will swing back—the one that, in the Third Industrial Revolution, pulled us away from our humanity and made us operate like machines. In order to work in the factories, people had to take jobs where they carried out the same tasks, repeatedly, as if they were robots. Those jobs have, by and large, been automated out of existence. Now that more intellectually-oriented jobs are being automated, too, we can anticipate being restored to ourselves and each other. Gone altogether will be the model under which factory bosses and other bosses squeezed all that they could from their workers, only to toss them aside and hire replacements as soon as they felt the time was right. Any vestige of similar principles at work in the white-collar world will soon be gone. Leaders who want their companies to stay afloat will have to treat their employees well, and imbue their work with a sense of purpose and dignity. This will coincide with our liberation from the current drudgery of so much of the work we do, and give us the freedom to work toward causes that truly matter.

Think again of Silicon Valley—of a company like Facebook, the development of which was motivated by a desire to bring people together and help them communicate more easily with one another. It would be hard to miss how the company has fallen short of achieving this, or the mistakes it has made on its way to achieving its vision. But such grand disruptions will motivate many more companies, and many more of their employees, in the days to come.

This shift will coincide with dramatic changes to the way we live and work. We will shrug off many of the current stressors of the workplace, of the uncertainty of livelihoods and reputation-building. We will have a firmer grasp of just where we stand in the working world at large and with the companies that employ us more specifically; on the other hand, we will have a clearer sense of what we need to do to make ourselves better performers. This will free us to focus on the purposeful work that needs to be done, that gets us fully engaged and drives even better performance. We will be in a far better position to live as we prefer to, to do the things that matter to us, and to truly seize the day.

CHAPTER SEVEN:
Carpe Diem

I WAS BORN IN 1966, on the dividing line between one generation and the next. I have been working all my life, and have seen firsthand how dramatically workplaces and working life have changed in the last thirty years. Computers redefined the way we worked; email revolutionized how we interacted in and out of the office; fax machines came and went; and smartphones made it possible to be available at all times, to communicate and collaborate regardless of location.

Even having lived to see these dramatic changes, I am certain that I have only an inkling of the changes that are ahead. AI will bring with it a revolution on an order we have not seen before; I don't even know quite what to compare it to, what historical precedent there might be for what is coming. The cotton gin is not quite comparable; it affected only agricultural work. Desktop computers are not quite similar, either; they only changed the ways in which we work, not who got to keep their jobs, nor how decisions were made that affected those people's livelihoods.

The changes are coming, and fast. Some know this very well, and have acted on it. By the time I left Microsoft, not long ago, people making seven figures were giving up their careers, there and at other companies, in favor of a new approach to their work and their lives. They abandoned promising careers in favor of working as consultants, escaping workplaces many of them found constraining or unsatisfying.

They did this because they could; their expertise was and is still in high demand. They did it, too, because they knew the old ways are going by the wayside. They saw the future coming, and acted accordingly.

These people are not aberrations; they are simply the first to act on a trend that is sure to grow. Many of the people who have not done as they have will find themselves going in the same direction soon.

On both ends of the payroll spectrum, people have the same needs and concerns. They want more control over their work and their lives. They want to be able to sustain themselves and find some real value in living. The latest generation of people to enter the workplace expect more than their parents and grandparents did, from what they do and from their work environments. It isn't just about a paycheck anymore.

If employers want to attract talent like theirs, they need to change the environment. Millennials and members of Generation Z are turning their backs on toxic workplaces, stalled paychecks, bullying managers, and low-innovation environments. Large companies will have to adapt and be creative to attract and retain talent as there are new ways of engaging with work, creating value, and finding self-fulfillment.

We should see this present moment as a great opportunity, living as we are on the cusp of radical changes. Good things are ahead, and we should embrace them—at the same time that we work hard to correct the shortcomings of the world we live in and make it better.

A THOUSAND MOZARTS

I was talking with my wife, recently, about the massive accumulations of wealth we have all witnessed among tech entrepreneurs.

It really is quite staggering, the sums of money they have—my wife agrees with me on this. Some of the billionaires have enough money to start their own private space programs, and they have done exactly that. Soon they are likely to be trillionaires, and I have little faith that their interest in space is quite the same as what we see in the scientists at NASA. I wonder if they are there to do research, and to expand the sum of human knowledge—or if they simply want to show off, or do it for the sake of being the ones to do it, or to distance themselves from the messy lives of those of us here on Earth.

Jeff Bezos was recently quoted as saying that the human race will need to populate other planets in the next 200 years. If we do not, he says, "'we'll eventually end up with a civilisation of stasis, which I find very demoralising… The solar system can easily support a trillion humans. And if we have a trillion humans, we would have a thousand Einsteins, a thousand Mozarts and unlimited resources.'"[74]

I don't know for certain what Bezos means by a "civilization of stasis"—except, perhaps, that the concept of stasis might itself be anathema to someone whose company has only grown since its inception. For Amazon, perhaps, to stop growing is to begin to die. I do not know whether the same rules apply to whole civilizations.

It could be that that isn't what he means, but I am skeptical of his enthusiasm for having "'a thousand Einsteins, a thousand Mozarts, and unlimited resources.'" Billions of people have lived and died since Mozart and Einstein came and went, and we have still had only one of each of them; meanwhile, a staggering number of the billions of not-Mozarts and not-Einsteins who have passed through this life have gone hungry, died of preventable diseases,

---

74 Hannah Schwär. "Jeff Bezos says his most important work isn't Amazon." *Business Insider.* April 27, 2018. *http://www.businessinsider.com/jeff-bezos-most-important-project-isnt-amazon-2018-4* (accessed June 12, 2018).

and/or struggled through their daily lives without any sense of fulfillment or satisfaction. If Bezos has a plan for ensuring that a trillion people, scattered among our solar system's planets, all but one of which has no breathable atmosphere, have enough to eat and aren't totally miserable, he has not come forward with it.

And it is not only Bezos who dreams of space travel, and has the resources to act on his dreams. He is famously locked in a private space race with Elon Musk, who now has a car, manufactured by his company, in orbit around our planet. Richard Branson has a private space program; his focus is on space tourism for the rich. Tickets are expected to cost about a quarter-million dollars.[75]

Private companies working on space exploration is nothing new; what is new, as Alan Yuhas explained, writing in The Guardian, is that private companies are exploring space with their own goals in mind, rather than taking their cues from NASA and other government entities. "'What's new is that the companies themselves have ambitions beyond government contracts,' said Casey Dreier, director of space policy at the Planetary Society, an advocacy group. He compared it to the Gilded Age, when billionaires sought to single-handedly reshape the future, or at least the marketplace, for good or ill."

Musk, Bezos, and Branson are competing with one another to decide the future of space travel; other wealthy men, with companies of their own, have joined the competition. Jeff Manber, CEO of Nanoracks, plans to build a private space station. He has said, "'We want to be part of a society moving to space.'"[76]

I worry—and I know I am not the only one who worries this—that the soon-to-be-trillionaires' enthusiasm for space travel is not exactly in our best interests. It concerns me that when they envision a new society in space,

---

75 Christian Davenport. "The Unsung Astronauts." *The Washington Post*. June 15, 2018. *http://wapo.st/unsungastronauts* (accessed June 18, 2018).

76 Alan Yuhas. "The new space race: how billionaires launched the next era of exploration." *The Guardian*. February 9, 2018. *https://www.theguardian.com/science/2018/feb/09/new-space-race-billionaires-elon-musk-jeff-bezos* (accessed June 15, 2018).

there may not be much or any room for the rest of us. It seems likely enough that they mean to get as far from the rest of us as they can and not bring us with them.

Writing in The New Yorker, Evan Osnos described members of the superrich upper-upper-class who have their own personalized underground bunkers, private islands with carefully curated arsenals, helicopters they keep gassed up in case they need to escape all the rest of us, and houses in New Zealand, where they think they will be safe in the event of an apocalypse that claims everyone except for those who can afford to get away from it.[77] The superrich spacemen, with the cars they launch into space, might have the very same motives as these earthbound tycoons with slightly shallower pockets and no spaceships to speak of; their goal might merely be to get far away from the rest of us before things start to get very bad.

If that is the case—and I'm not certain that it is; I hope it isn't—it is a serious shame. Their wealth is vast. They could do with it any number of things that would be unquestionably good for a great number of people.

They are not merely wealthy men; they are leaders. They are public figures. If they simply decided to do so, they could help make inequity a thing of the past, or at least help us make some enormous first steps toward achieving that goal. You might go so far as to say they have a responsibility to do that, to make their vast wealth serve the greater good.

They deserve credit for doing this, when they do it, like when Jeff Bezos pledged $2 billion to build preschools and provide aid to homeless families.[78] Bill and Melinda Gates, and Warren Buffett, would seem to agree that they have a responsibility to put their wealth toward good causes, as they have spent many millions of dollars to promote the causes they believe in.

---

77 Evan Osnos. "Doomsday Prep for the Super-rich." *The New Yorker.* January 30, 2017. *https://www.newyorker.com/magazine/2017/01/30/doomsday-prep-for-the-super-rich* (accessed June 12, 2018).

78 Elizabeth Weise. "Amazon CEO Jeff Bezos announces $2 billion fund to build preschools, help homeless families." *USA Today.* September 13, 2018. *https://www.usatoday.com/story/tech/science/2018/09/13/amazon-ceo-jeff-bezos-announces-2-billion-charity-fund/1289788002/* (accessed November 17, 2018).

Indeed, it is not as if the other billionaires and multimillionaires lack examples they could follow.

I, for one, have no interest in saving up for a private island I can run to when things get bad. There is too much work to do to prevent things from getting bad in the first place—too much good we can do with and on behalf of the people who make up our society. And we have far too much to look forward to.

MAKING OUR WORKING LIVES WORK

Good things are in store for us. Life will only get better.

I know that may seem like a delusional statement, made in a fog of imperceptions and sheer oblivion, given the current state of our politics. At the time of writing, the dominant political party is protectionist, bellicose, and anti-immigrant; in order to see good things taking place, when we look around, we have to squint hard to see past the immediate calamities that play out before us.

But the calamities will not last forever. Nothing does. And it is within our power to help bring an end to them soon, and start to turn the social and political tide in our favor. We can take actions to make things better in the present and begin to build a brighter future. We can do this today. We must do it.

We must not work only for the 1 percent. We must reorient our collective goals so that we work for the common good at least as much as we work for the benefit of billionaires. If we do not change course in this way, if we do not reinvest in infrastructure and education, and do all that we can to increase healthy competition among businesses, the result will be more than my own personal disappointment. It will mean the United States further relinquishing its role as a leader in the world, and the engine that drives the Fourth Industrial Revolution.

In trying to achieve this, my primary focus is on how to improve our working lives—how to speed the process of phasing out vestigial routines and structures that trap us as soon as we enter the workforce and refuse to let go. So many people are working nine-to-five jobs in static offices, with fluorescent lights glaring down at them, their every move watched by someone, presumably—and all of this at a time when we have within our reach technology that can replace that dynamic with one that is far more suitable to us. Not only is it within reach, it is in daily use already. There is no need for anyone to be so confined, and the spaces in which we work deserve to be transformed, just as the substance of that work will be.

There is so much unhappiness, and so much of it is unnecessary. I want to take the subjective conversations people have all the time, about the shortcomings of their working lives, and make them objective. I am developing a way to make unfortunate workplace conduct, like discrimination, backstabbing, and unproductive forms of competition, into things of the past. I want to take the kinds of data collection that have been in practice for years and turn them to our collective advantage, bringing people together who are open to new ideas and willing and ready to collaborate. I want to empower good leaders.

This is what I am doing. And there is more for us all to do—so very much more.

We need to regulate our industries, across the board—reinforce the regulations that have been threatened by recent political activity, and establish regulations for those that are new enough not to have been properly reined in.

My thinking on this is focused on the world of technology, because it is the world I have worked in, the one I know best, and the one I know has gone sorely underregulated. Perhaps that is because it is still relatively new; perhaps it's also because the prime movers of the tech industry have donated to the right politicians or otherwise managed to fly under the regulatory radar. But this industry has gotten far too large for it to not be given the same kind of scrutiny we give to the automobile industry, nuclear power, and so many other things. As we have all learned, it does not take much neglect or outright nefariousness, in order to precipitate real damage to our democracy and social fabric. The Cambridge Analytica scandal will only be the tip of the iceberg, unless we can establish limits and regulations on data collection and other such practices.

I should reiterate, for the sake of clarity, that despite my enthusiasm for regulation, I am no socialist. I have always worked in the private sector. I have thrived there. I invest in companies and am bringing one of my own into the world. By calling for regulation, I am not advocating for an over-throw of our current economy.

What I want is to ensure its long-term survival—to guarantee that it functions as well as possible, by seeing to it that those who are in power establish and enforce sensible rules that foster competition. We have to ensure that blood circulates to all of the extremities of our society, and the way we do that is to ensure that it doesn't pool in any one part—meaning that we cannot let a handful of companies or individual people become too powerful, as they currently threaten to.

I am not the first to observe that monopolies currently threaten to dominate whole industries. Others have begun to take action to stop this consolidation of wealth and power. Progressives have taken it on as an urgent matter and a worthwhile issue, and I read recently about Lina Khan, Director of Legal Policy at the Open Markets Institute.

> Khan and her colleagues at Open Markets think the current anti-trust standard lets big corporations dominate the industries they're in. "We've been living through an experiment, and the results are all around us," says Khan, who rejoined Lynn's organization after Yale. There are four major US airlines and three major drugstore chains, and mega-retailers like Walmart and Amazon have the power to dictate terms to their suppliers.[79]

Khan is one among many who are ready and willing to begin to break up monopolies and put dormant antitrust laws to good use. She is part of a

---

79 Robert Levine. "Antitrust law never envisioned massive tech companies like Google." *The Boston Globe.* June 13, 2018. *https://openmarketsinstitute.org/clippings/boston-globe-antitrust-law-never-envisioned-massive-tech-companies-like-google/* (accessed June 18, 2018).

nascent movement led by the Open Markets Institute, a small but influential Washington-based think tank, is trying to reverse several decades of court decisions in order to bring the law back to its Progressive Era roots... Rather than focus on consumer pricing, or even consumers at all, these New Brandeis thinkers want to preserve competition itself.[80]

One example of an acquisition this group no doubt took an interest in, the likes of which it might do more to halt in the future, came when Microsoft recently acquired Github for more than $7 billion.

Github is well-known among developers as a forum for open-source project development, a virtual space where programmers can go to share their innovations and tweaks to existing software. While many have hailed Microsoft's acquisition of Github as a positive development, I—and many others—see in it a disastrous turn of events.

Windows as a paid OS has not survived the fierce competition from Apple and Google, especially in the mobile space. And it is suffering to live with no or low interest from developers who could bring relevant innovation. By purchasing GitHub, they are trying to get closer to the developer community and influence their development innovation toward its own products. To survive, Microsoft has to embrace open source—what was once the resistance. Those are signals of the new era, where open platforms based on collaboration will prevail. Large companies will have to learn how to harness that creative potential and share profits with the larger community. That is worthy of paying $5 billion more dollars than its actual value. It is the price of survival.

In paying that price, they have limited competition. They have made the free market less free. It is the opposite of what, as good capitalists, we should stand for, and it is exactly the sort of thing we should insist our representatives in Congress put a stop to. It becomes more urgent all the time that we do this, as enormous companies continue to acquire other companies, growing bigger than ever, eliminating competition, and ruling out

---

80 Ibid.

any possibility of fairness in a free marketplace. As David Leonhardt wrote in The New York Times, companies like Disney, Comcast, Verizon, and a handful of others "have decided that their best strategy for raising profits involves getting bigger. Larger companies simply have more power — to compete with other giants, to restrain workers' pay, to influence government policy and, in the long run, to increase prices." This has had a long-term negative impact on the lives of everyday people; Leonhardt ends his article by writing that "corporate consolidation is a problem that's within our power to fix. A government that wanted to reduce the power of big business — through a combination of new laws, better regulation and different judicial appointments — could do so. Here's hoping we get such a government sometime soon."[81]

If we act right, we can ensure that this government comes into being. We can look forward to a time when our experience of virtual spaces—which is, by now, so bound up in our overall experience of life—is enriched by the constant competition between companies that are proportional in their resources and capabilities. We have been deprived of this for so long, it is hard even to picture what that would look like.

NET NEUTRALITY AND NEW REGULATIONS

In order to ensure that this competition is even possible, we need to reinstate net neutrality. The loss of it will have dramatic, negative effects that have yet to play out fully. To this day, I am baffled that the decision to end it was made—that, despite the vast number of people who use the Internet, and who have come to rely on it working the way that it does, Ajit Pai, Chairman of the Federal Communications Commission, ended net neutrality, and made it possible for large, moneyed corporations to consolidate power over what gets communicated to whom and at what price. I am convinced that this only came about because too many people in Washington do not grasp

---

81 David Leonhardt. "The Charts That Show How Big Business Is Winning."
The New York Times. June 17, 2018. https://nyti.ms/2JXJxs9 (accessed June 18, 2018).

its full implications.

Those who are responsible for the decision like to downplay the effects of what they have done, saying we should not overreact, and insisting that things will not change very much, if they change at all.

Indeed, we may not notice many of the incremental changes. We will be like the proverbial frog in a pot of slowly boiling water, who does not feel every minor increase in temperature, but still ends up getting boiled to death because someone is slowly cranking up the temperature.

We must reinstate net neutrality through legislation, rather than leave this tremendously important facet of our digital lives up to the whims of a single regulatory body. The FCC has far too much control, in this case, over something that affects the lives of too many people—which includes virtually anyone who uses the Internet on a regular basis.

Rather than continuing to leave regulation in the hands of agencies that were established long before the invention of the Internet, we need to rethink regulation.

On the one hand, it is tempting to imagine new agencies, created by Congress, that could better regulate highly technological markets and new technologies. This would mean our government establishing new high-tech agencies that serve as watchdogs against dodgy practices on the part of tech companies, like data mining. They could help prevent the next Cambridge Analytica scandal, implement plans for providing high-speed Internet access to all Americans, and begin to prepare us for the rise of AI and the potentially massive bite it will take out of our job market.

A change to how we regulate new and recently minted technologies is absolutely in order. The digital revolution has swept through our lives, changing everything: how we work and how we play, the way we communicate with business associates and our closest friends. Technologies that once promised to help us order a pizza with the click of a button have made our lives unrecognizable from what they once were. But the regulatory bodies we count on to help decide policies that concern these technologies are many decades old.

It is time for us to address the shortcomings of current regulations, but new regulatory bodies are not necessarily the solution. We can do even better than that. We can write our regulations into the very code of the computer programs and algorithms that govern so much of our lives, and make this a requisite aspect of newly developed software.

It's not about having a group of people who create rules; people can be corrupted, or replaced by the already corrupt. The end of net neutrality is a fine example of how things can go wrong when we give fallible human beings too much control over regulation and rulemaking.

We can forego the need for regulatory agencies altogether, as they pertain to new technologies, by making all the new software self-regulating. We can build code into algorithms, going forward, that will protect against the infractions we deem to be most important, and thus rule out the possibility that special interests might influence those who run regulating agencies and render them ineffectual. It is imperative that we do this, to ensure that automation works on our collective behalf and not against us. Experts can implement self-controlling units inside each system that gets produced for use by the public. This way, regulations can be scalable; they can adjust automatically to match the size and scale of the things that are being regulated.

And, lest I excite the enmity of anyone who is, on principle, deeply opposed to regulation, consider the observation by the Open Markets Institute that "concern about the costs of public regulation" only serve to

distract...the public from the costs of private regulation. Dominant actors with market power are often able to set the terms within a specific marketplace, thereby dictating outcomes for other businesses. Such unilateral exercise of private power is also very much a form of regulation. As Robert Hale wrote, "There is government whenever one person or group can tell others what they must do and when those others have to obey or suffer a penalty." Especially in digital technology markets, certain dominant firms now exert regulatory control over the terms on which others can sell goods and services.[82]

According to this line of thinking, there is no such thing as a total absence of regulation; a lack of governmental regulation only means that it is up to industries and companies to regulate themselves—something that we, as citizens, have absolutely no say in, as elected officials have no influence over the process. I prefer to have a system in which there is some form of accountability.

WHAT WE NEED TO PROTECT OURSELVES AGAINST

When the regulations I am describing are instituted—and I have every confidence that they will be, sooner or later—there are three areas they need to cover, three boxes that must be checked if they are to do us any good.

The first box is personal identifiable information (PII), which consists of any information that can be traced to us, or that is directly relevant to us. This includes social security numbers, phone numbers, credit card numbers, and our names—anything that is specific to us and that can be exploited by those who want to commit fraud or simply use that information to their advantage and not ours.

This information must be protected; we have caught a glimpse of what can happen when we do not protect it, with the Cambridge Analytica scandal showing how much manipulation can take place using information that is quite limited in its scope.

Protecting our PII is important not only because it can be used to subvert our democracy; it is a question of privacy. And we have seen how sweeping new regulations can be, on this point; the European Union adopted rules regarding online privacy, and everyone who frequently visits websites was

---

82 "Public Comments of the Open Markets Institute Submitted to the Antitrust Division Roundtable Examining the 'Consumer costs of Anticompetitive Regulations.'" *Open Markets Institute.* May 31, 2018. *https://openmarketsinstitute.org/commentary/ public-comments-open-markets-institute-submitted-antitrust-division-roundtable- examining-consumer-costs-anticompetitive-regulations/* (accessed June 18, 2018).

flooded with emails outlining new terms of service. Companies all over the world that operated online had to adopt the new rules, not only in Europe, but for everyone, worldwide. The European Union showed us that regulations can be imposed on tech companies across the board, and that they can be effective.

The second box that must be checked, as this undertaking goes forward, is bias. We must protect ourselves against unfair bias, and this protection must be written into the systems in which bias threatens to work against us.

There are any number of ways bias can be built into the systems we rely on and work against us. Here is one example.

Imagine you have a machine learning process that creates offers, on behalf of hiring managers, for the new employees they intend to hire. The algorithm ventures out, researches the market, learns average salaries for comparable positions, and compares a candidate's education and work history against those of others. It does all of these things automatically, almost instantaneously, and provides the hiring manager with a preloaded job offer, an ironclad salary and benefits package that cannot be negotiated because the system has determined it is ideal; it is the best offer that candidate will get. This will happen; it will be something like the advent of fixed prices for used cars; what once was negotiable is decided according to exact data and can hardly be challenged.

Here is where bias comes in. The algorithm will no doubt pick up on the fact that women tend to be paid less than men. Unless it is programmed to do so, it will not recognize this disparity as a stark injustice. It will simply internalize that data and act accordingly. And so the algorithm that creates these offers on the part of hiring managers will perpetuate the unacceptable trend of women being paid less than men; it will render it automatic, etching that disparity into stone.

It will do that, anyway, unless we take this seriously and impose rules on the companies that create such algorithms, stipulating that antibias code must be written into every pertinent program. Rather than perpetuate bias, we can halt it, once and for all.

This can be done. It will require significant mobilization on the part of those of us who care about this and want our lives to get better—but it is perfectly attainable.

I am confident that measures like this one will be taken; it is only a matter of whether we will wait for a crisis like Cambridge Analytica, or something larger than that, to come and go, or if we will take measures to prevent such a thing from taking place.

The third box that we must check, as we go about keeping tech companies and their innovations in check, is perhaps a slipperier one than the first two; it encompasses all of the many ethical considerations we must take into account as technologies develop. With every new app and algorithm comes vast potential for abuse and manipulation. We have to guard against it at every turn.

To offer one example, my car insurance company recently emailed me to say that, if I downloaded onto my phone an app they had created, I might be eligible for a reduction in my insurance premium. It sounded, on its surface, like a good enough deal—doing something that would hardly impact me would save me money.

What that app would do, of course, is track my location at all times and determine what sort of driver I was. If I ran red lights, stole the right-of-way from other drivers, or consistently drove well over the speed limit, then the car insurance company would know it and presumably act accordingly—raise my premium, or keep it where it was.

That may still sound like a fair enough deal, a new incentive for people to drive safely. But the algorithm could take any number of factors into consideration as it determined whether or not I was a safe driver. I might park my car in a neighborhood where vandalism tends to get reported more often than in other places—where cars are keyed or otherwise maligned, resulting in insurance claims that the company would have on record. If I went there to visit a friend, or get a stereo repaired, or whatever I wanted to do, and the app tracked that I had gone there and left my car parked for a while, I might find that my premium had gone up—simply because I went gone to a part of town that my car insurance company's automated system frowned upon.

If I lived in that neighborhood, the effect would be far worse; my car would spend much more time there, putting it at greater risk, meaning my rates would be more likely to go up, or would increase more sharply.

Since this frequent vandalism I refer to is far more likely to be a trait of lower-income neighborhoods than high-income areas, this effect would be felt much more greatly by those who live in low-income neighborhoods, and who themselves have low incomes. This would create a regrettable disparity in insurance premiums for the rich or middle-class and the poor, reinforcing already stark income disparities and obliterating any chance at improving equity.

This same logic extends to technologies that could and probably will soon track our health. My health insurance company might offer to lower my premium if I keep track of what I eat, what groceries I buy, and how often I get sick. I might begin to do this voluntary work in the hope of saving some money; maybe, because I tend not to buy junk food, or because I cheat a little bit and don't report the junk food I buy, my premium will drop slightly (though, at the same time, such reporting will by that point be automatic, if Amazon's new supermarkets—which have no cashiers, and which charge you for your purchases automatically—catch on). Then, perhaps I'll catch the flu and get a series of colds throughout the following year. I might report this, in the name of total honesty, not thinking that the algorithm that tracks my health and reports on me to the insurance company will take this to mean that I have a poor immune system. It might couple this news with the fact that I am not as young as I used to be. I might find that my insurance premiums increase unexpectedly, and without any indication as to why.

This would not exactly be fair. I would have a problem with it. And it's another scenario in which technology would work against the poor, who by and large have less ready access to or cannot afford food like fresh vegetables, let alone organic produce and grass-fed meat products. It's hard to eat well when you don't have much money—but unless we dictate that an algorithm must take something like this into consideration, and behave ethically, it will not. Technologies that might appear to mean well—or that mean well very genuinely—could turn out to be quite destructive and only further strain our social fabric.

This is where we must focus our energies: not only on developing new technologies, but ensuring they are implemented in a way that increases equity and does not only further push the rich and the poor farther from one another. We absolutely cannot afford to do that.

Once again, I have every confidence that these regulations will be put in place—that we will determine that new systems like I have described must enforce ethical limits and rules as automatically as they do everything else. The question is whether we will wait to see how much damage can be done without such self-regulating programming before we implement it.

We have already felt, and will continue to feel, the effects of not having properly regulated the use of PII. The fact that we haven't regulated well, or created self-regulating mechanisms, jeopardizes our democracy and makes identity theft and other, smaller crimes, more likely.

We can easily identify the next frontiers of coding. We must create pieces of code that everyone has to include on their software, to protect against bias. This can be done, and it is something that governments must require.

This is where we come in; this is where we can take action, and begin to demand that our government take action, scrutinizing the doings of the newest tech companies and those that have not yet been founded. We need people who fully grasp the workings and implications of new developments like data collection to communicate the dangers to those in power—namely, our representatives in Congress—and articulate for them what can be done to avert catastrophe.

The new technologies are far too powerful and influential for their power and influence—and that of their inventors—to go unchecked. It is up to us to give voice to these concerns, and put pressure on elected officials who are in a position to act on them.

They will not consider this a priority unless we convince them to do so. This is where persistence becomes essential, and familiar tactics become very useful, like calling and writing to our representatives, and electing to office those who are technologically savvy and willing to impose new limits on what we allow tech companies to do.

I am not at all the first person to stress the need to regulate new technologies. Oren Etzioni, chief executive of the Allen Institute for Artificial Intelligence, wrote in the New York Times in 2017 about how we might go about regulating artificial intelligence. Taking his cue from Elon Musk's urging that AI be regulated, Etzioni outlined three fundamental rules that must be imposed on AI: "First, an A.I. system must be subject to the full gamut of laws that apply to its human operator...My second rule is that an A.I. system must clearly disclose that it is not human...My third rule is that an A.I. system cannot retain or disclose confidential information without explicit approval from the source of that information."[83] This, he explains, will help to keep AI within acceptable limits of ethical behavior; the establishment of these rules will prevent a human whose AI representative behaves illegally from defending themselves by foisting blame onto the AI.

It would be a good start, to have such rules in place. That we have not done even this much, or anything close to it, should indicate how unprepared we are for the changes AI will bring with it.

Other countries are getting up to speed. As Alan Boyle reported in *Geekwire*, "the United Arab Emirates already has a minister of state for artificial intelligence, and that the British government is funding a Center for Data Ethics and Innovation. Chinese and French leaders have also talked up government-led AI initiatives." He quotes Kay Firth-Butterfield, a policy expert, as saying, "'With this technology moving so fast, we're very often in what could be called the 'too late' zone," she said. "By the time we've legislated, the horse is four or five fields down the lane.'"[84] This is absolutely correct, and

---

83 Oren Etzioni. "How to Regulate Artificial Intelligence." *The New York Times.* September 1, 2017. *https://www.nytimes.com/2017/09/01/opinion/artificial-intelligence-regulations-rules.html* (accessed June 14, 2018).

84 Alan Boyle. "Policy experts trade ideas for intelligent ways to regulate artificial intelligence." *Geekwire.* April 10, 2018. *https://www.geekwire.com/2018/policy-experts-debate-regulate-artificial-intelligence-intelligently/* (accessed June 14, 2018).

while it can be refreshing to read the words of someone who so clearly gets it—who sees what the problem is and understands its urgency—that brings us no closer to actually reckoning with the imminent problems that AI will bring with it.

Reading about the potential for AI regulation, few writers or experts address the full effects of AI, the job losses and workplace disruptions that will do us good, in the end, but impose terrible losses in the short term. There is no plan, currently, for addressing those fractures.

We have an agency in place that can, when properly administrated, rush to the scene of a destructive hurricane—but we have no plan in place for what to do with out-of-work truck drivers and project managers when they are replaced by robots and they must be reeducated if they are to continue to work. There will be many thousands of them, they will need help, and they will look for answers to why there isn't any. We must do something about this. We do not even have a plan for preventing unfair biases from being adopted by the new automatons; this is an egregious oversight, and it is up to us to correct that.

We must do it in the name of equity, since, at the end of the day, that is what is being threatened. When people lose their livelihoods, and their fields of work go by the wayside, they will be shut out of the economy without any means for getting back into it. It will mean making an unfair world less fair, and a hard world to live in even harder to live in. To continue to take no action on the changes that are to come is not only unwise, it is inhumane.

THE CHILDREN

As I am a father, I cannot leave off further emphasizing how important it is to put limits and regulations in place, given that our children will inherit any mistakes or oversights we make. And as things stand, we are committing many of them, potentially leaving it to them to clean up our mess. There is no excuse for this.

But there is far more to the plight of children in our rapidly evolving technological landscape than this. Young people take to social media readily, discovering new ways of expressing themselves there that go far beyond the limits of how they are in person. It can be hard to control young people's access to the digital world; I, for one, would not dream of restricting absolutely my kids' access to new technology. Young people today are native to technology in a way that is really quite remarkable to those of us who grew up in a world that did not even have desktop computers in it.

One deeply tragic illustration of this facility with new technologies on the part of the young was what we all witnessed in the wake of the Parkland High School shooting. In the wake of a mass murder, the survivors took to social media to tell their stories and champion measures that would prevent such atrocities from taking place in the future. It is old news by now, but people were genuinely stunned by this; there had been school shootings before, but we had never seen its survivors respond so swiftly. It was, as many noted, a sign of a generational shift, the induction of a generation of young people who grew up with social media into a horrid tragedy.

I do not want to risk sounding in any way enthusiastic about the terrible events that played out in Parkland. I used to live very near to that school; I have connections to the community, and like so many others I am, to this day, stunned by what played out there.

I hope that the technologies that make possible new forms of communication, and increased connectedness between people, allow us to find new solutions to old problems. I am always hopeful that something good can spring from the worst possible calamity. It is for that reason that, despite all of the harm that new technologies can do, and have done, I feel strongly that children should have access to new technologies, that they should have the opportunity to take to them as if they were second nature.

That is, more or less, what they do, when given the opportunity. Many of us have seen how readily a small child can learn to use a smartphone, learning swiftly from observing their parents or others how they can scroll with it, and zoom in and out. There are risks involved with children's use—and overuse—of technology, but a child today starts out life in a world where smartphones, with their instant access to the Internet, have preceded them. This can be a great advantage for them, as they immediately master new technologies that often take their elders much longer to figure out.

We often hear the opposite—that we should restrict our kids' access to technologies of recent vintage. Many profiles have been written of one pair or another of Silicon Valley denizens who deny their children access to the Internet—a move that is presented to us all as a cautionary story of what people who know how the sausage is made think of the sausage they're making.

As Chris Weller wrote, in Business Insider, of the couple Minni Shahi and Vijay Koduri,

> The Koduris' life is that of the quintessential Silicon Valley family, except for one thing. The technology developed by Koduri and Shahi's employers is all but banned at the family's home.
>
> There are no video game systems inside the Koduri household, and neither child has their own cell phone yet. Saurav and Roshni can play games on their parents' phones, but only for 10 minutes per week. (There are no limits to using the family's vast library of board games.) Awhile back the family bought an iPad 2, but for the last five years it's lived on the highest shelf in a linen closet.

This is meant to give us all pause, and make us wonder: just what is it that these insiders seek to protect their children against? What do they know that we don't know?

But upon closer inspection, we learn that they know only what most parents do: that too much of anything is bad for children, and that excessive use of smartphones and tablets, not unlike excessive television watching, isn't good for them. "Koduri and Shahi represent a new kind of Silicon Valley parent," the article goes on. "Instead of tricking out their homes with all the latest technology, many of today's parents working or living in the tech world are limiting — and sometimes outright banning — how much screen time their kids get." But this is, more or less, exactly how many parents manage their children's access to screens. And it is nothing new. But because these families' Internet deprivation needs to come across as sensational, articles like this one include details that make child management sound a little foreign, with details on someone like Taewoo Kim, "chief AI engineer at the machine-learning startup One Smart Lab… A practicing Buddhist, Kim is teaching his nieces and nephews, ages 4 to 11, to meditate and appreciate screen-free games and puzzles. Once a year he takes them on tech-free silent retreats at nearby Buddhist temples."[85] The management of children's screen time is given this eccentric sheen so that we miss that it is reflective of an altogether ordinary approach to childrearing in the twenty-first century.

It isn't hard to find guides for raising children in a world rife with smartphones and other such things. A common approach is to allow children access to digital technology, but to both monitor and regulate that access and model restraint; parents who are glued to their phones will raise children who are glued to phones. We are encouraged to steer our children toward creative, rather than consumptive, uses of technology; this discourages passivity.[86] It can be helpful to have such rules pointed out to us, but they are fairly commonsense ideas.

I am no proponent, however, of offering children unfettered access to all that new technologies have to offer. Social media in particular offers substantial risks to kids' well-being, and the most obvious reasons are perhaps not the most important ones. The Kaspersky Lab identifies the greatest risks of children's social media use to be "Reputation damage, cyberbullying, [and] pedophilia." Further down the list are fraud, malware, and exposure to inappropriate content.[87] These are grave threats indeed, and should be taken

---

85 Chris Weller. "Silicon Valley parents are raising their kids tech-free – and it should be a red flag." *Business Insider.* February 18, 2018. *http://www.businessinsider.com/silicon-valley-parents-raising-their-kids-tech-free-red-flag-2018-2* (accessed June 18, 2018).

86 Joshua Becker. "9 Important Strategies for Raising Children in a World of Technology." *Becomingminimalist. https://www.becomingminimalist.com/ikids/* (accessed June 18, 2018).

87 "The Dangers of Social Networks." The Kaspersky Lab. February 26, 2016. *https://kids.kaspersky.com/the-dangers-of-social-networks/* (accessed June 18, 2018).

seriously. Parents have been warned about them since the days of AOL, Prodigy, and CompuServe.

But the aspects of social media I worry about most are more subtle and insidious than that; they are the same qualities that threaten the wellbeing of the grownups who use it. Social media can be a great facilitator of positive change; it can be a lever people use to topple dictatorships. It can also be a destructive whirlpool of bad habits and genuine harm.

A report cited in The Independent states that "While eight- to 10-year-olds use social media in a 'playful, creative' way – often to play games," older children who use social media hover precariously over an abyss that threatens to destroy their self-images, or at least badly distort them. "The study suggests some children are becoming almost addicted to 'likes' on Facebook and Instagram as a form of social validation, with many increasingly anxious about how they appear online."[88] I would not wish this on any children—or grownup for that matter. But I trust that adults have strong enough senses of themselves that such effects would not do lasting damage. I cannot say the same for children.

While they are awfully informative, it is not even necessary to look at studies of effects on children of social media to understand the harm they can cause. Anyone who has used social media for more than a few hours knows the unique sort of awfulness that can spill out of it, the strange way an ill-meaning or even well-meaning post by someone you know can worm its way into you and fester there. Exposure to social media is fraught at best, because social life is fraught at best; being among people always involves some hurt, some discomfort, some embarrassment or anger. When children experience that in virtual spaces, they go through it in a kind of mitigated isolation; they can be caught helpless and unaware.

We grownups are still only beginning to understand the dangers of social media and teaching ourselves to manage its presence in our lives. It

---

88 Mary Bulman. "Children facing 'significant emotional risk' on social media, report warns." *The Independent.* January 4, 2018. *https://www.independent.co.uk/news/uk/home-news/facebook-children-risk-emotional-impact-report-warning-a8140526.html* (accessed June 18, 2018).

only stands to reason that we should manage our children's access to it; I, for one, have forbidden my children to use it.

But social media is only one dimension of today's technologies; otherwise, I ensure that they have ready access to computers, smartphones, and tablets. It is hard for me to imagine living without these things; it will be even harder for them, in years to come. I have every reason to ensure they are familiar with these things, early in their lives; as with so many other potentially harmful things, I am only careful to ensure moderation.

THE GOOD NEWS

Even given the pitfalls that lie ahead of us, we are headed for a bright future. We are in the midst of an industrial revolution. They tend to be chaotic at best, but amidst the chaos will arise great benefits.

This is the Fourth Industrial Revolution, after all; there have been three prior industrial revolutions we can learn quite a lot from.

The First Industrial Revolution made us dreamers. The possibility of automation made us dream of a new future for humankind—liberated from so many unsavory forms of labor, we were able to think bigger than before, and hope for far better things than ever.

The Second Industrial Revolution brought us the combustion engine and electrification—the effect was to make us all super-rational. The Third Industrial Revolution made us more productive than ever; with the inventions of the computer, and the advent of the Internet, we were compelled to act more and more like machines, to do our work with degrees of precision and efficiency not seen before. We have been judged according to our output first, and everything else has followed.

Now, with the Fourth Industrial Revolution, something new will be possible; released again from so much difficult labor, we will be free to realize our full potential as human beings. Our leisure or discretionary hours will only increase, having grown dramatically since 1880. This has given rise to whole industries, like the entertainment industry, which had almost no place in prior eras. Entertainment is something we engage in far more often and for longer periods of time than the average person would have 200 years ago; today, many people think nothing of investing forty hours, eighty hours—sometimes 400 hours—in playing a computer game.

Of course, though, with the continued rise in leisure hours comes the need to use them wisely. If we want to be part of the future, we cannot spend all of our leisure time playing the latest installment of *Fallout* or *Minecraft*. Such activity will only become less tenable as education becomes something we are expected to engage in on a self-paced, ongoing basis. An app like Duolingo, which I discussed at length earlier, demonstrates the way in which learning and leisure can go together; we can expect to see more of this, and find novel ways to merge education with entertainment.

While that may not sound supremely appealing now, it will, once we begin going to work because our sense of purpose compels us to do so, rather than our need to keep ourselves fed. When our work is done collaboratively, in the name of a unifying cause, it will be second-nature to us, to want to keep ourselves educated, to self-improve voluntarily.

We already do our fair share of this. Health clubs would hardly be as lucrative as they are if that were not the case. But whereas it is now an admirable trait, continued self-education and self-improvement will soon be expected of us; we will have to do it, in order to stay relevant in a world that continues to change.

One of the great opportunities, with the implementation of AI, is for companies to invest more than ever in the people they still need when much of the work we do is automated. When companies employ fewer people, and the positions that survive mass automation are more specialized, companies will have to work harder to retain their employees; they will have to make people want to work for them. Leaders and human resources departments will need to rethink how to treat their workers, and what constitutes a sustainable, bearable, equable, and thriving workplace.

We are familiar with some of the imagery of this—of colorful, wonderfully sunlit offices in Silicon Valley, where coders and engineers are invited to take frequent breaks from work to play table tennis and enjoy the complimentary juice bar. These images are familiar enough to have been satirized on TV and in movies. The tech workplace always seems to be portrayed as either a hotbed of innovation or an unserious place, a frivolous playground for overpaid youngsters wearing shorts and t-shirts who are too smart and rich for their own good.

Whether those images are truly reflective of the Silicon Valley culture is questionable; if you ask an employee of Google or Facebook, they might well have a stockpile of complaints to draw on that have nothing to do with the popular perception of where and how they work.

But the potential for a better workplace—and better world—is not limited to the increase of amenities for those who are employed there. And many of the measures that companies can take are well within reach, like ensuring that, in the absence of a social safety net, employees are provided with benefits and wages that are well above livable.

Companies in Silicon Valley already embody much of what we can expect from the future of work, like jobs that provide not only steady paychecks but a sense of purpose. There are more ways in which they can lead the way toward the work of the future, which will improve our lives in the future.

We have spent time, throughout this book, on the changing meaning of leadership, and the expanding role of the leader. The best, most inspiring, most successful leaders will be those who understand the need to shape the future at the same time that they shape their individual companies.

SEIZE THE DAY!

Our lives have improved dramatically since the First Industrial Revolution. The Fourth will continue the trend that began so many decades ago. We will enjoy quantities and forms of leisure that were unheard of in eras past; there are truly great things ahead. But we cannot sit back and simply expect the new world to come into being on its own.

As the world changes, we will change with it. We will, and must, come to worship, as a society, something other than money. We must find the right balance between the pursuit of our livelihoods and living our lives; we must ensure that the economic system that pulled us out of the dark ages does not plunge us into another one, with the worst of what climate change has to offer on its way and our ways of addressing it now so insufficient.

It is up to us as individuals to seek solutions to big problems and live as best we can. It is up to the companies we work for to do the same, and facilitate the better lives we strive for.

We must do all that we can to ensure that we win little victories that take us in the right direction—that the representatives we vote into office, and the things we urge them to do, support sustainability and social equity. We need to do all that we can—but there is only so much we, as individuals, can do. Not only will we soon do all of our work collaboratively; we must collaborate as we shape the world we spend the rest of our lives in, and which our children will inherit from us.

We must have social equity and the livelihood of many people in mind. We must find a way to better distribute wealth and see to it that no one is left behind as we continue to move forward. We must conjure bold visions of a better future, and do all that we can to help make those visions into reality, working in the name of sustainability, democratization, and humanization.

We need to live in the moment and work between those moments. We need to understand that everything is fluid, that we live in the midst of great change.

We must make the best world we can, and seize the day.

SINCE I WAS A LITTLE KID, I have always dreamed about building speaking robots and time travel. As I grew up, I kept nurturing my passion for technology becoming an electronic engineer. In 1989, as part of my graduation, I took part in one of the first academic teams developing AI in Brazil, and my team mission was making a robot see and recognize objects. We learned fast that making the robots see was easy but, the recognizing part would still take a few decades to be done. I changed gears and my interest quickly swung to understanding human sciences. I found in Strategic Marketing a good way to learn and explore. I have dedicated almost three decades to help large enterprises add up a few billions of dollars to their top line with innovative concepts and products, and more importantly, developing a good understanding of human behavior. The expertise and experience developed in working with leading tech companies, allowed me to cross the fields of human sciences and technology and empowered me to become a futurist with a broader perspective including economy, sociology, philosophy, and technology. I still cannot time travel, but I do have glimpses of what the future will look like and what we have to do today to build a better future. Now AI is in full development and I am leading a new tech company that uses AI to empower humans in the new workplace. I have been dedicating part of my time to raise awareness about important decisions we have to make today, to build a future where all of us can thrive.